D0319836

THIS BOOK SHOULD BE RETURNED ON OR
DATE SHOWN TO THE LIBRARY FROM WHI

N.W.R.L.
BIRKENHEAD
Due 3/3/92

LANCASTER LIBRARY
MARKET SQUARE
LANCASTER LA1 1HY
Tel 63266

30.
21. APR 92
26. JUL
01.
08
21. DEC 93
18. APR 94
02. JUN 95
19. JUN 95
04.
18. APR 96
18. JUN 96
05 AUG 96
11. OCT 96
31 JAN 1997
18. 09. 97
22. 10. 97

AUTHOR
DELFONT, B.

CLASS Shelve at
792.7 B/DEL

TITLE
Curtain up':

Lancashire County Council
THE LANCASHIRE LIBRARY.
Library Headquarters,
143, Corporation St.,
PRESTON PRI 2TB.

a30118 050436157b

Curtain Up!

The Story of the Royal Variety Performance

Lord Delfont

Robson Books

05043615

First published in Great Britain in 1989 by Robson Books Ltd,
Bolsover House, 5–6 Clipstone Street, London W1P 7EB

Copyright © 1989 Entertainment Artistes' Benevolent Fund
Compiled for the EABF by Complete Editions Ltd

British Library Cataloguing in Publication Data
Delfont, Bernard
Curtain Up!
1. Great Britain. Variety shows to 1988
I. Title
792.7'0941

ISBN 0 86051 629 6

All rights reserved. No part of this publication may be reproduced, stored in a retrieval system, or transmitted in any form or by any means, electronic, mechanical, photocopying, recording or otherwise, without the prior permission in writing of the publishers.

Typeset by Bookworm, Manchester
Printed in Great Britain by Butler and Tanner Ltd.
Frome, Somerset

ENTERTAINMENT ARTISTES' BENEVOLENT FUND

Patrons

Her Majesty The Queen
Her Majesty Queen Elizabeth The Queen Mother

Life President
Lord Delfont

Hon. Chairman
Roy Hudd

Vice Chairman
Philip Hindin

Hon. Treasurer
Peter Prichard

General Secretary
Reg Swinson, M.B.E.

Life Governors

Rt. Hon. the Earl of Derby, M.C.
Lord Delfont
Serge Ganjou
Louis Benjamin
Billy Marsh
Richard Tompkins

Vice-Presidents

Ken Dodd, O.B.E.
Lonnie Donegan
Jack Jay
Peter Jay
Danny La Rue
Nat Mills
Ronald Smart
John Street
Ronald Swift
Norman Teal
Frankie Vaughan, O.B.E.
Ben Warriss

Executive Committee – 1989/91

Leslie Adams
Peggy Ashby
Wyn Calvin M.B.E
Joe Church
Lord Delfont
Pat Dodd
Robert Earl
Peter Elliott
Serge Ganjou
Philip Hindin
Vera Hindin
Roy Hudd
Lew Lane
Len Lowe
Laurie Mansfield
Ninette Mongador
Billy Moore
Alf Pearson
Bill Pertwee
Peter Prichard
Jack Seaton
Don Shearman
Charlie Smithers
Don Smoothey
John Street
Harold Taylor
Bruce Trent
Bert Weedon
Bob West
Billy Whittaker

Trustees
Lord Delfont, Jack Jay, Ronald Smart, Sir Harry Secombe, C.B.E.

Bankers
Midland Bank Ltd.
Charing Cross Branch
455 Strand
London WC2 0RH

Consultant Architect
Kenneth Stott, A.R.I.B.A.

Solicitors
Caporn, Campbell
5 Brighton Road
Surbiton
Surrey

Matron
Mrs. R. Campbell-Watson
S.R.N.

Medical Advisor
Dr. Alex Hall M.B.Ch.B.
Dr Graeme Robertson
M.B.Ch.B., D.R.C.O.G.,
D.A.M.R.C., G.P.

Brinsworth House
72 Staines Road, Twickenham TW2 5AL

Acknowledgements

The author and publishers would like to thank Bill Pertwee for the extensive help he gave in the compilation of this book. In particular, for permission to quote from his book *By Royal Command*.

The majority of the photographs in this book have been generously supplied by Roy Hudd and Lew Lane from their own private collections. Thanks are also due to the Raymond Mander and Joe Mitchenson Theatre Collection for permission to reproduce the following photographs: Max Bygraves, page 89; The Beatles, page 134; Michael Flanders and Donald Swann, page 135 and Frankie Howerd, page 145. We are also grateful to Doug McKenzie and his daughter Penny at Professional Photographic Services for their patient help.

FOREWORD
by Lord Delfont

As Life President of the Entertainment Artistes' Benevolent Fund it is both an honour and a source of great pride to present this history of the Royal Variety Performance, which celebrates its Diamond Jubilee this year and has in the course of this century established itself as a unique and hugely popular British institution.

My own involvement with the Royal Variety Performance dates back to 1958, when I presented my first 'royal show' at the Coliseum. Robert Nesbitt joined me that year as my director, a role which he continued to perform throughout the next two decades as year after year we strove to compile shows that reflected the broad and ever-changing spectrum of entertainment. To him, the EABF and I owe a lasting debt for the consistently high standards of direction and innovation that he brought to bear in staging a show that, in its early days at least, relied on a bare forty-eight hours of rehearsal and drew artistes from the four corners of the globe.

In 1958 I was also joined in this work by Billy Marsh, one of our most respected show-business managers and a Life Governor of the Fund. For the next thirty years he was to act as an invaluable adviser on every Royal Variety Performance and he remains one of its mainstays today, as well as a greatly respected figure in all branches of show business.

After twenty years I decided that the time had come to pass the reins of leadership on to our Vice President, Louis Benjamin, who had long been associated with the intricacies involved in the months of planning and preparation. Under his sure guidance, the Royal Variety Performance continued and accelerated its progress as the sole annual variety show that commands a worldwide audience.

Louis Benjamin, with the able assistance of his director, Norman Maen, struck out into new ground by constructing several shows around immensely successful themes. This brought a freshness and vitality that appealed to both the audience in the theatre and the increasingly important television audience at home and abroad.

On a financial level the Royal Variety Performance under Louis Benjamin made far-reaching advances as well, and these underpinned and secured the increasing expenditure of the EABF in its important work of caring for retired and elderly members of our profession. Between 1979 and 1984 he more than trebled the Fund's income from the Royal Variety Performance and, judged artistically and financially, his years as presenter will remain major milestones in the history of both the Fund and the show.

We are fortunate in having on the Executive Committee some of the most fertile and dynamic brains in modern show business, and when the growing complexity and cost of staging the Royal Variety Performance, coupled with the key role that television now plays, brought about a further realignment, we had in Laurie Mansfield and Peter Prichard two members of the Committee ideally qualified to set the Fund and the show on a firm and profitable course for the 1990s and beyond. Under their inspiration and instigation the BBC and ITV now alternate as presenters of the Royal Variety Performance, relieving the Fund of all financial responsibility and ensuring a consistent and profitable income for its charitable work for the years ahead. To Laurie Mansfield I owe a special thank-you, for it was he who first suggested the idea of compiling this book.

Throughout its history, as our Chairman Roy Hudd explains in his own Foreword, the Royal Variety Performance has been the major fund-raising event of the EABF and in this respect the General Secretary has always played a pivotal role. In the early years Harry Marlow occupied this important position and did much to foster the inestimable links between the Fund and the Royal Family. He was succeeded after more than forty years by Arthur Scott, who furthered his predecessor's work before he too handed over, in 1968, to the present holder of the office, Reg Swinson. Throughout the last twenty years, which have been characterized by such important and fundamental changes, Reg has kept a steady hand on the tiller, helping to steer the Fund through the mounting inflation of the late 1970s, while still developing and extending its all-important work. He has cheerfully given up a great deal of his time to offer invaluable assistance and a large measure of practical help in the compiling of this book, and when he officially retires in June next year the EABF will be losing one of the loyalest, most diligent and conscientious officers it has ever had in its distinguished history.

Without question the principal factor that perpetuates, enhances and extends the reputation and global success of the Royal Variety Performance is the Royal patronage the Fund has been honoured to be graced with for so many years. The presence of the Family each year sets the seal upon all the glory, the endeavour and the purpose for which the Fund has worked in the past and will continue to work in the future. In the Diamond Jubilee Year of the Royal Variety Performance it is my very great privilege to offer the Royal Family, on behalf of all who have been associated with the work of the Fund, our enduring gratitude.

Lord Delfont
September 1989

FOREWORD
by Roy Hudd

First, thank you for supporting the Entertainment Artistes' Benevolent Fund. The Royal Variety Performance is for the benefit of the Fund; it is our major fund-raiser.

After the first royal show, in 1912, King George V said he would attend a once-yearly variety show provided the profits went to the Variety Artistes' Benevolent Fund, as the EABF was then known. Our Royal Family has never failed us since.

The thousands of pounds the show has raised have been wisely spent. We have improved and

enlarged our residential home, Brinsworth House in Twickenham, till only the façade of the original nineteenth-century building remains and we have brought practical help to thousands of performers, young and old, from circus, cabaret, clubs, theatre, radio and television.

The RVP, as it is affectionately referred to, has always mirrored public taste in light entertainment, but it is more than that. As you read through the unbelievable lists of names, you'll see reflected the history of our Islands: the names that cheered and inspired us in bad times, the names that heralded the birth and development of radio and television, and the names that shaped popular music.

To a performer a Royal Variety Performance is the great accolade and certainly the most nerve-wracking 'gig' he or she will ever tackle. I have had the ecstasy and the agony four times and, believe me, it gets no easier. I remember passing a young comic backstage doing his first. I said 'How are you feeling?' He said 'I've walked round the outside of the theatre fifteen times rehearsing my four minutes. How are you?' I said, 'I'm just off on my twentieth lap!'

Everybody suffers, yet it is the one show nobody turns down. They come from all over the world, free, gratis and for 'nowt', just to help their less fortunate brothers and sisters. It makes you very proud to be a member of that exclusive collection – the 'pros' who are the characters in the continuing story of the Royal Variety Performance.

Roy Hudd
Hon. Chairman, The Entertainment Artistes' Benevolent Fund
September 1989

1 July
Palace Theatre, Shaftesbury Avenue
In the presence of Their Majesties King George V and Queen Mary
Presented by Oswald Stoll
Musical Director – Herman Finck

THE PROGRAMME

Pipifax and Panlo – Eccentric Act 'Humpsti Bumpsti' **Barclay Gammon** – Pianist
The Palace Girls in 'A Fantasy in Black and White' after Phil May
Chirgwin – 'The White-Eyed Kaffir' **The Bogannys** – 'Five Minutes in China Town'
Fanny Fields – 'The Happy Little Dutch Girl' **Paul Cinquevalli** – 'The Human Billiard Table'
Harry Tate – Motoring sketch **Ida Crispi & Fred Farren** – 'Everybody's Doing It'
Vesta Tilley – 'Algy, The Piccadilly Johnnie' **La Pia** – Dancer
Little Tich – 'The Gamekeeper' – and his Big Boots
Arthur Prince and 'Jim' – Ventriloquist act
Alfred Lester assisted by Buena Bent – 'The Village Fire Brigade' sketch
Clarice Mayne – Singer
Charles T. Aldrich – Quick-Change Character Actor and Juggler
George Robey – 'The Mayor of Mudcumdyke' **David Devant** – – Magician
Wilkie Bard – 'Want to Sing in Opera' **Anna Pavlova** and Members of the Imperial Russian Ballet
Harry Lauder – Singer
Cecilia Loftus – 'Impressions of Artistes' 'Variety's' Garden Party,
featuring 142 members of the variety profession

(*Note: This was the programme as published, but on the night, due to running time and other constraints, some changes had to be made.*)

1912

This was the very first Royal Command Performance in the Art of Variety, and must still rank as one of the most successful. The previous year there had been a Royal Command Performance, at Drury Lane, but that was for the so-called 'legitimate' theatre. In 1912 all the great names of British variety and music hall gathered at the Palace Theatre before King George V and Queen Mary. All, that is, apart from Marie Lloyd, perhaps the biggest name in popular music hall at the time. Her omission – apparently on the grounds that she was too *risqué* for such a Royal performance at a time when music hall was just becoming 'respectable' – is one of the most controversial in the history of the Royal Variety Performance.

Her absence, however, failed to dampen the excitement of a memorable night of British entertainment, with stars such as comic Harry Lauder, Harry Tate, the 'Prime Minister of Mirth' George Robey, dancer Anna Pavlova and the 'White-Eyed Kaffir' G.H. Chirgwin ensuring a triumph.

The Performer was certain about the success of the show. 'We must frankly confess that we are not in the Royal confidence,' it wrote, 'but nothing, so far as outward manifestation could prove, could have been more obvious than the pleasure the King and Queen and the rest of the Royal party . . . took in the long variety programme presented to them.'

It continued: 'Perhaps the highest compliment His Majesty could have conveyed was his confession to Mr Alfred Butt, who with Mr George Ashton had the honour of receiving and bidding farewell to the Royal party, that he had apprehended too long a performance, but that, on the contrary, he had thoroughly enjoyed every detail.'

The Stage, too, said that, while the show would enjoy financial success, 'this was as little compared with the fact that Royalty, in the persons of the King and his Consort, have officially set their seal of approval upon the work of that large body of people who are to be found in what is comprehensively termed the variety profession.'

And Mr Wal Pink, a member of the organizing committee, said simply: 'The music hall has come into its kingdom.'

Sadly, with war clouds gathering, the second Royal Variety Performance had to wait for another seven years.

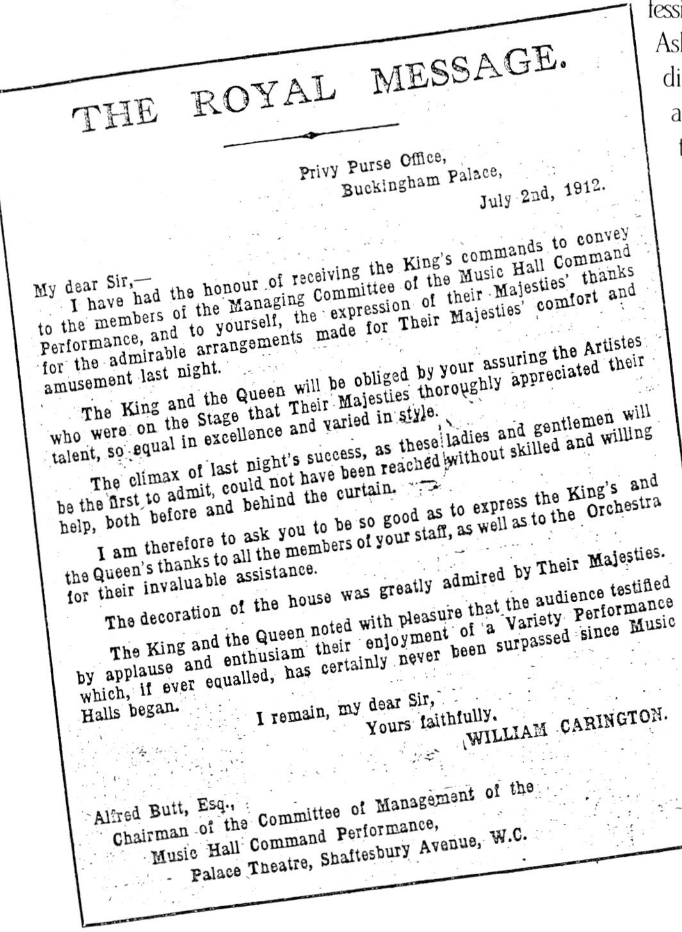

THE ROYAL MESSAGE.

Privy Purse Office,
Buckingham Palace,
July 2nd, 1912.

My dear Sir,—

I have had the honour of receiving the King's commands to convey to the members of the Managing Committee of the Music Hall Command Performance, and to yourself, the expression of their Majesties' thanks for the admirable arrangements made for Their Majesties' comfort and amusement last night.

The King and the Queen will be obliged by your assuring the Artistes who were on the Stage that Their Majesties thoroughly appreciated their talent, so equal in excellence and varied in style.

The climax of last night's success, as these ladies and gentlemen will be the first to admit, could not have been reached without skilled and willing help, both before and behind the curtain.

I am therefore to ask you to be so good as to express the King's and the Queen's thanks to all the members of your staff, as well as to the Orchestra for their invaluable assistance.

The decoration of the house was greatly admired by Their Majesties.

The King and the Queen noted with pleasure that the audience testified by applause and enthusiam their enjoyment of a Variety Performance which, if ever equalled, has certainly never been surpassed since Music Halls began.

I remain, my dear Sir,
Yours faithfully,
WILLIAM CARINGTON.

Alfred Butt, Esq.,
Chairman of the Committee of Management of the
Music Hall Command Performance,
Palace Theatre, Shaftesbury Avenue, W.C.

1912

There was one moment of unease, when Vesta Tilley, the talented male impersonator, began her act. Queen Mary, seemingly unhappy with the idea of a woman wearing trousers and dressing like a man, covered her face with her programme, which encouraged the audience to be less enthusiastic in their reception to Miss Tilley. Fortunately, a following act was the great comic, Harry Tate, and his ability to get George V laughing soon restored the lively atmosphere.

Even a seasoned performer such as Little Tich could be overawed by a grand occasion. Things started well for him as he sang 'Popularity', a well-known 1910 number, and then went on to do his famous 'Big Boots' dance. It was towards the end of the night that Little Tich was overcome with nerves and, very sadly, found himself unable to join in the grand finale.

Vesta Tilley

Harry Lauder

Eager to have a special reminder of the evening, Harry Tate told his son Ronnie to go up to the Royal Box after the show to see if a programme had been left there by the Royal party. He was in luck – Ronnie found the specially hand-embroidered one given to Queen Mary, a real collector's item.

Alfred Lester was literally caught with his pants down by the Prince of Wales. After the show, the Prince came back-stage, eager to say how much he had enjoyed the performance. Unfortunately, Lester was in the middle of changing – with very little to cover his blushes. The distraught entertainer is quoted as crying out, 'It's awful – I can't shake hands with my future sovereign in my pants and vest.'

LITTLE
TICH
DAVID
ALLEN & SONS
LTD
BELFAST
ONE TICH OF NATURE
MAKES THE WHOLE WORLD
GRIN
DAVID
WILSON

28 July
The London Coliseum
In the presence of Their Majesties King George V and Queen Mary
Presented by Oswald Stoll
Musical Director – Alfred Dove

THE PROGRAMME

The Flying Banvards – Comedy Stage Gymnasts
Ernest Hastings – Humour and Music at the Piano
George Robey and **Violet Loraine**
Sam Barton – The Comedy Man with a Bike
Arthur Prince and 'Jim' – Ventriloquial Comedy
Harry Tate – 'Selling a motor car'
Clarice Mayne and 'That'
Grock, the Famous French Clown, and Partner
Du Calion – 'The Loquacious Laddie on the Tottering Ladder'
A Pageant of Peace by Louis N. Parker, with
Ethel Hook and Company. Orchestra conducted by Sir Edward Elgar

1919

This second 'royal show' was staged as a celebration of peace and, as the official announcement expressed it, had been commanded by the King 'to show his appreciation of the generous manner in which artistes of the variety stage have helped the numerous funds connected with the war.'

The finale was a particularly moving piece entitled *A Pageant of Peace*. There was a large chorus portraying the Allies and the Colonies. In one scene, six hundred women clothed in white fanned out from the flight of steps. Four trumpeters from the 1st Life Guards blew a fanfare before Sir Edward Elgar conducted music arranged by the appropriately named Mr Dove. Then from the top of the white steps at the rear of the stage descended Ethel Hook as Britannia to herald the singing of 'Land of Hope and Glory' before the National Anthem.

Harry Tate

Despite the overall success of the show, there were some complaints from commentators about the 'coldness' of the audience which inhibited some of the performers. 'A possible explanation is that this was the outcome of a mistaken sense of "etiquette" in the presence of Royalty,' said one critic.

George Robey

25 November
London Hippodrome
In the presence of Their Majesties King George V and Queen Mary
Presented by Oswald Stoll
Musical Director – Julian Jones
Stage Director – H.E. Bright

THE PROGRAMME

Frederick Sylvester & Co. – 'The Neatest of the Neat'
Norah Blaney and **Gwen Farrar** – Ragtime Burlesque
G.S. Melvin – The Versatile Comedian
Renée & Godfrey – England's Leading Young Dancers
Malcolm Neil McEachern – Singer
Rebla – A Comedy Episode
'The Valley of Echoes' scene from *The Peep Show* with **Annie Croft, Reginald Sharland, Fred Allandale, Albert Darnley, Ruth French, Mary Gibbs**
W.H. Squire – Violoncellist
Lilly Fairney – Vocalist
Auriol Jones – Pianist
Gabriel-Marie – Cellist
Herbert Oliver – Vocalist
Ella Retford – Comedienne
Milton Hayes – The Laugh-Smith with a Philosophy
Billy Merson – The Star Comedian
The Five Petleys – Aerial Comedy

1921

The previous Royal Command Performances had been 'one-offs', but the 1921 show was the first of the more regular performances. It was the brainchild of Mr Harry Marlow, organizer of the Variety Artistes' Benevolent Fund, to establish a regular series of shows, and his idea was warmly welcomed at Buckingham Palace. Indeed, George V, a great fan of music hall, agreed to become life patron of the VABF – the start of an unbroken line of Royal patronage until the present day.

There were some fears that the public might not respond so well and at first tickets sold slowly. But the timely announcement of Princess Mary's engagement to Viscount Lascelles, and the news that their first public appearance afterwards would be at the Hippodrome, guaranteed a full house.

A feature of the evening was the recital by Milton Hayes of his own verse, *The Book of Variety*. Another star was bass Malcolm Neil McEachern.

The evening raised £2,000 for the VABF – including £50 which the King himself gave for the Royal Box.

Ella Retford

1921

An act which gained the King's particular applause was G.S. Melvin's hornpipe. It was said that during his naval career George V had been very partial to performing a hornpipe himself.

Billy Merson was one of the best comedy acts of the night. His hilarious antics in the musical comedy pieces brought roars of laughter from the audience.

G S Melvin

Milton Hayes, dubbed the 'Laugh-Smith with a Philosophy', seemed to be in great favour with the Royal party. In addition to reading from his *Book of Variety*, he gave a send-up of political propaganda, which was rated one of the funniest turns of the evening.

Billy Merson

Milton Hayes

12 December
London Hippodrome
In the presence of Their Majesties King George V and Queen Mary
Presented by Oswald Stoll
Musical Director – Julian Jones
Stage Director – H.E. Bright

THE PROGRAMME

The Flemings – Artistic Creations in Alabaster
Will Fyffe – The Scottish Comedian
Kharum – The Persian Pianist
Du Calion – 'The Loquacious Laddie on the Tottering Ladder'
Lorna and Toots Pounds – Entertainers
P.T. Selbit, illusionist – 'Sawing Thro' A Woman'
Muriel George & Earnest Butcher – Old Folk Songs
Tom Webster – Animated cartoon 'Tishy'
Arthur Prince and 'Jim' – Ventriloquial playlet
Harry Weldon – Comedian
Trix Sisters – Singers
The Mirthful Jovers – Comedians

1922

The Queen of Norway joined the Royal Party for this year's show, which for the second year running was at the Hippodrome. Their Majesties were treated to a cast list generally agreed to be more varied than that of the previous year.

Arthur Prince, who had appeared in the very first 'royal show', was again a big hit with his ventriloquist act, ably assisted by his dummy Jim. Their interpretation of the 'Love Affair of Yussif Hassan' drew a large round of applause.

A further oriental note was struck by Kharum, described as 'The Persian pianist from the land of Omar Khayyam'. His dexterity at the keyboard was greatly admired. He could play popular melodies of the day intermingled with Chopin, and amused the audience hugely with one tune played entirely with his left hand.

The Scots comedian Will Fyffe was another great success, especially with his rendition of 'a hardy old farmer' who sang lustily about being 'ninety-four today'.

Rather more unusual, but equally popular, was a cartoon show called 'Tishy' created by Tom Webster. He was in the stalls during the showing of the film about the crazy horse's adventures, but was called on stage with enthusiastic acclaim at the end to receive the justly earned applause for what proved to be an immensely popular item.

And, in keeping with the traditions of variety, the Flemings provided a strong-man act that certainly appealed to His Majesty.

Muriel George and Earnest Butcher

Will Fyffe

13 December
London Coliseum
In the presence of Their Majesties King George V and Queen Mary
Presented by Oswald Stoll
Musical Director – Alfred Dove

THE PROGRAMME

Bobbie Hind and his all-British Sonora Band
Rupert Hazell
Katrina and Joan
The Griffith Brothers
Lola Karsavina
Sessue Hayakawa, Lewis Gilbert, Ann Trevor and **Dora de Winton in** *The Samurai*
Royal Albert Hall Orchestra, conducted by **Sir Landon Ronald**
Scene from *Brighter London* with **Billy Merson, Reg Sharland, Eddie Jaye, Bernard Dudley, Laddie Cliff** and **Rena Hall**
Russian Blue Bird Players
Alfred Lester
Loie Fuller Ballet
Marimba Band
'The Disorderly Room' with **Tom Walls, Ralph Lynn, Tommy Handley, Jamieson Dodd, Cecil Bainbridge** and **Fred Kemp**
Nothing to Do, finale by **Louis N. Parker**

1923

By 1923 the Royal Variety Performance was already becoming established as a major event in the world of entertainment, and this year there were few problems selling tickets for the Coliseum.

As usual the theatre was brightly decorated for the occasion. And the effect was enhanced when, as the King and Queen and the rest of the Royal entourage entered their box, thousands of electric fairy lights came on, lighting the whole auditorium, while the band played the National Anthem.

The show, which lasted two and a half hours without an interval, was notable for a one-act play by William Archer called *The Samurai*, with Lewis Gilbert and Ann Trevor. The idea of 'straight' theatre, and also ballet, mixing with variety and music hall acts was gradually becoming more and more popular on British stages.

Another hit was the comedy sketch 'The Disorderly Room' by comedian Tommy Handley, later a star of radio.

More exotic offerings were provided by the Marimba Band of Guatemala and the Griffith Brothers and Miss Lutie and 'their remarkable performing horse Pogo'.

1923

The impact of the Great War was still uppermost in people's minds, and in the spirit of the time the Prince of Wales made a generous donation to provide seats for ex-servicemen who had been wounded on active service.

The honour of appearing in a Royal Variety Performance is perhaps somewhat diminished by the fact that it is as the hindquarters of a grey horse! This was Fred Griffith's claim to fame at any rate, though he had in fact appeared before Royalty in a more recognizable form in 1886.

Ralph Lynn

Tommy Handley

12 February
Alhambra, London
In the presence of Their Majesties King George V and Queen Mary
Presented by Oswald Stoll
Musical Director – George M. Saker

THE PROGRAMME
George Hurd
Mr and Mrs Tree
Will Hay
Ethel Hook
Milton Hayes
J.W. Jackson's Twelve English Dancers
G.H. Elliott – The Chocolate-Coloured Coon
Will Fyffe – The Scottish Comedian
Nervo and Knox
Talbot O'Farrell – Singer
Harry Tate and Company

1925

It was a night of laughter at the Alhambra for the Royal Variety Performance, with comics such as Harry Tate, Scotsman Will Fyffe and Will Hay having a great impact. As the *Morning Post* reported, 'One has never known a performance of the kind go so well; no audience ever enjoyed itself more . . . altogether the merriest evening of its kind.'

As well as humour, the King and Queen were treated to a true variety of acts from 'mentalism' to juggling and light opera.

The juggler, George Hurd, can once scarcely have imagined that one day he would be appearing in front of Royalty – at the age of eleven he was working on a sheep farm in the outback of Australia!

A popular musical act was G.H. Elliott, the so-called 'chocolate-coloured coon', who blacked up for his act in days when such things were quite acceptable.

Overall, the evening passed off well. *The Performer* remarked: 'That the Royal visitors did thoroughly enjoy the performance there was not the slightest shadow of doubt.'

Nervo and Knox

1925

Audience participation was alive and well in 1925 as the act of Mr and Mrs Tree amply proved. While Mr Tree moved among the audience inviting them to whisper their choice of music in his ear, his blindfolded colleague, seated at the piano on stage, would immediately begin playing the requisite tune – musical requests by 'thought transmission'.

At this year's Royal Variety Performance, Mr Tree climbed into the Royal Box to ask the King to choose a popular air. His Majesty whispered that he would like to hear the overture to *The Merry Widow*. No sooner had he spoken than the popular melody was struck up by Mrs Tree on stage.

One of the proud traditions of the Royal Variety Performance is that so many shows have presented opportunities to young performers starting on the ladder of show business, many of whom have become household names as a result of one night of success. In 1925 the laurel fell on a young comedy duo named Nervo and Knox, among the youngest performers on the cast list. This was the first appearance in a Royal Variety Show of the two evergreen comics who were later to swell the ranks of the celebrated Crazy Gang.

Their inclusion was perhaps something of an educated guess as King George V was well known for enjoying the slapstick humour of artistes like Arthur Lucan and Kitty McShane.

Then as now, performers took great pride in being part of show business. The singer Talbot O'Farrell, a former cabinet maker and soldier who worked his way up the hard way, remarked at the time of the show: 'I am satisfied that this profession is the best in the world, if one cares to take it seriously, and remember that we are all, from managing director to call-boy, part and parcel of a great industry, and are, after all, responsible for our success and greatness to our customers – the wonderful British public.'

Mr Tree

Mrs Tree

27 May
Alhambra, London
In the presence of Their Majesties King George V and Queen Mary
Presented by Oswald Stoll
Musical Director – George M. Saker

THE PROGRAMME

The Twelve Famous John Tiller Girls – Dance Troupe
Dick Henderson – The Comedian Who Sings
Robb Wilton – Burlesque scene 'The Magistrate'
Lillian Burgiss – The English Ballad Singer
Jack Hylton and His Famous Band
Conn Kenna – 'The Funny Airman'
Carr & Parr – Dancers
Bransby Williams – Selections from Dickens
The Houston Sisters – Musical Sketch
Billy Bennett – 'Almost a Gentleman'
Rich Hayes – Exploring with 'Man Friday' on Crusoe Island

1926

Up until 1926 the only way to get a taste of the unique atmosphere of such a night was to queue for a ticket. For it was this year that the first-ever broadcast was made of the Royal Variety Performance. It was, of course, on radio, and to overcome the potentially awkward silences during visual acts broadcasters would provide 'commentaries' on the performances, rather like modern-day sports commentators.

Certainly the – at that time – small radio audience and those at the Alhambra enjoyed an evening of rich variety. There were comedians Robb Wilton and Dick Henderson, dancers Carr and Parr and a leading ballad singer of the time, Lillian Burgiss, who 'enthralled' the audience with her version of 'The song that reached my heart'. Jack Hylton, in later years a successful producer and manager of the Crazy Gang, and his Band were the first variety orchestra to appear in a Royal Variety Performance. In fine fettle that day, they played, among other numbers, 'Laughterland', 'Rose Marie', 'Babette', and 'Bam Bam Bammy Shore'.

WEEK MAY 24, 1926 - PAVILION, LIVERPOOL

BRANSBY

WILLIAMS

MAY 27, 1926

ALHAMBRA

ROYAL PERFORMANCE

Before Their Majesties

The KING & QUEEN

DECEMBER, 1906

Personally Commanded to appear at Sandringham by His Majesty

KING EDWARD VII

Before Her Majesty Queen Alexandra, Prince and Princess of Wales (present King and Queen), etc. Presented by His Majesty with a Royal Souvenir.

BRANSBY WILLIAMS

230, Finchley Road, Hampstead, N.W.

Bransby Williams

1926

A point of interest is that none of the performers in the 1926 Royal Variety Performance had appeared in any of the six previous shows. *The Stage* described the programme as 'a good working bill' considering the self-imposed desire to have an all-British and new cast. In 1970 almost the same criteria applied, with only one of the cast (Max Bygraves) having appeared before in a 'royal show'; everyone else was making their début.

Notable among the 'newcomers' of 1926 were the Tiller Girls and the comedian and singer Dick Henderson – father of the later star of Royal Variety Performances, Dickie Henderson. With a bowler hat too small for his head, he personified the myth of the 'jolly fat man' and won over the audience with consummate ease.

Sir Oswald Stoll, who presented the show at the Alhambra, earned praise from *The Performer* for his efforts. The newspaper pointed out that because of the General Strike there was a chance that the Royal Variety Performance might have to be switched from the Thursday to the Saturday, thereby losing Sir Oswald the Alhambra's normal lucrative receipts for that night. Although this was not necessary in the end, Sir Oswald with 'characteristic generosity' was 'quite prepared' to allow the switch. *The Performer* went on to say, 'There are few men in show business who have with so little ostentation or attempt at seeking the limelight achieved the prominence of Sir Oswald Stoll.'

Fear and anxiety have been the curse of many a performer's life. But spare a thought for friends and relatives who suffer the agonies at second hand! Billy Bennett describes how his mother was able to cope with the problem: 'My mother told me that as she sat in the circle and watched me she almost died lest I should forget my words, and she told me that she repeated them as they fell from me, to the amusement of the people sitting there.'

The Houston Sisters

This year's show revived hopes that music hall was making a come-back to the British scene, the *Daily Mail* writing of 'this essentially English institution coming into its own again'.

The Performer said of the show: '. . . that is one of the useful services rendered by such an event. It does help to bring variety into prominence out of the obscurity to which it has so unfairly been relegated by many of the newspapers.'

24 February
Victoria Palace, London
In the presence of Their Majesties King George V and Queen Mary
Presented by J.A. Webb
Musical Director – John Weaver

THE PROGRAMME

P.L. Clark – as 'Auntie'
Mona Grey – The Vari-Voiced Entertainer
Norman Long – With a Song, a Smile and a Piano
The Victoria Girls
Jack Edge – The Irresponsible
Debroy Somers and his Band
Albert Whelan – The Australian
Lily Morris – Comedy Character Songs
Georgie Wood with Dolly Harmer and Tom Blacklock in 'His Black Hand'
Mr Flotsam and Mr Jetsam
The Three Huxster Brothers

1927

The first Royal Variety Show at the Victoria Palace was enthusiastically received by the occupants of the Royal Box: 'An excellent performance – I cannot recall ever having seen a better,' the King remarked afterwards.

Indeed, His Majesty was seen to lean forward on a number of occasions from his box, as if anxious to get an even closer look at the acts.

These included impressionist Mona Grey, comedienne Lily Morris, Australian comic Albert Whelan and the singers Flotsam and Jetsam. Of particular amusement to the Royal Box was the comic song by Jack Edge, 'Could Lloyd George Do It?'.

Parts of the Victoria Palace show were broadcast on the wireless – eagerly listened to by residents of Brinsworth House. Writing in *The Stage*, a resident wrote: 'We had all looked forward to the great event, and the Superintendent Mr Thornton had seen to it that the fine four-valve wireless was in trim.

'There were fifty old pro's of ages varying from 55 to 90 years, anxiously waiting to hear our younger and more successful brother and sister artistes who were to entertain their Sovereigns.

'Old age has crept on the majority of us unawares and found us unprovided for, but thankful to God for the comforts and benefits derived from the efforts of our fellow-members of the profession, from a generous public, and for the wonderful lead given by Their Majesties.

'The orchestral selection of old-time airs was reminiscent of our own days of success. We were thrilled by the enthusiastic reception accorded by the audience to the Royal Visitors and the orchestra playing 'God Save the King' found us standing to attention.'

Mr Flotsam and Mr Jetsam

1927

The gifted mimic and elecutionist, Mona Grey, was not born with her talent, for it was not until the age of three that Mona began to talk. When her voice did finally come through, it endowed her with an extraordinary range that won her the sobriquet 'the vari-voiced artiste'. Her imitations of a loud-speaker, a gramophone, and a cheeky child, astonished and greatly amused the audience.

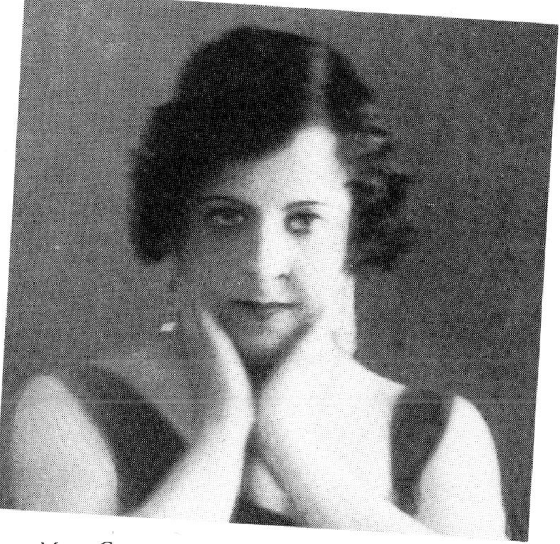

Mona Grey

Wee Georgie Wood

Wee Georgie Wood, described as the 'Peter Pan of the music halls', capitalized on his diminutive stature to give his act an unusual quality, and during his turn he took on all the characteristics of a naughty boy, which was reported as one of the major successes of the evening. The climax of his piece was the melodramatic 'sobbing scene' from *The Black-hand Gang*.

One of the highlights of the evening was the dancing of a twelve-year-old girl called 'Aeda', who came on during the playing of the Debroy Somers band. Dressed in sixteenth-century costume, she demonstrated with verve those rave dance steps of the day – the Charleston and the Black Bottom.

1 March
London Coliseum
In the presence of Their Majesties King George V and Queen Mary
Presented by George Black and Val Parnell
Musical Director – Alfred Dove

THE PROGRAMME

Larry Kemble – A Little Eccentric
Stanelli & Douglas – Fiddle Fanatics
The Victoria Girls
A.C. Astor – And 'Sentimental Mac'
Lillian Burgiss – An English Ballad Singer
Noni & Horace – Musical Absurdity
Victor André – The Unusual Dancer
Clarkson Rose – Comedian
Anton Dolin – Selected Dances
Gracie Fields – Comedienne
Will Hay and Company in a Comedy Sketch 'The Beginning of St Michael's'
Jack Hylton and his Band

1928

For years, it seemed, people had been proclaiming the death of music hall and variety. The 1928 show was one which put the lie to this.

The *Birmingham Evening Dispatch* commented: 'People who are always declaring that the music-hall performance is dead received rather a shock if they were at the Coliseum last night to see the Royal Command show in aid of the VABF. Throughout the evening, in fact, it was proved to the hilt that there is a real demand for variety, and that it is humour that the audience chiefly wants.'

The *Evening Standard* wrote: 'The Queen always enjoys these annual variety performances more than most theatrical events, and last night she laughed unrestrainedly at the mirth of what some people call the dying variety profession.

'For these few hours at least variety was very much alive.'

Anton Dolin

1928

The 1928 show was a signal success for the Variety Artistes' Benevolent Fund, raising £4,400 for the charity. When told of the amount, the King expressed his delight at the sum as well as his enjoyment with the evening.

And Will Hay spoke for many artistes when he expressed his gratitude to Their Majesties for their keen interest in variety. 'I feel very honoured,' he said. 'The royal support given to the variety profession every year is encouraging to all of us in vaudeville.'

One of the leading pantomime dames, Clarkson Rose, recalled how he quelled his nervousness with a little too much Dutch courage: 'After pacing up and down the dressing room for a while I went to the stage door for some air, and there was a well known agent in the vicinity who I knew. "Feeling a bit jumpy, are you?" he said. "I certainly am," I replied. He said, "Come out and have a drink, it will steady you up." . . . True it was only one whisky he had given me, but I think it must have been a treble, and I was not in the habit of taking a drink before my work. I heard my introductory music as if it were coming from a distance, and I walked on stage in a sort of trance. I sang my first song to only polite applause and quickly left the stage to change, ready for my second song. When I entered for that I slipped on the highly polished stage and up went my bustle, revealing my red bloomers!'

It seems he learnt his lesson from then on – 'It was the first and last time I ever took a drink before a show!

A leading daily commentary on the evening's entertainment said, 'Queen Mary was most amused with Clarkson Rose's delicious burlesque of a Victorian Dame, and the little trip he did, displaying voluminous underclothing caused roars of laughter led by her Majesty!'

Noni & Horace

Noni the Clown received the highly unusual accolade of receiving flowers from the Queen. Her Majesty sent him a stem from her bouquet, saying how sorry she felt when he confided that 'no one ever sent him flowers'.

The irony of life imitating art was of no comfort to Gracie Fields when she had to dash from her show to appear in the Royal performance. 'On the stage of the St James's where I am playing in *SOS*, I have to die,' she explained. 'I died in the usual way last night. Then I went over to the Coliseum to come as near dying of fright as I ever want to.'

1928

Gracie Fields

22 May
London Palladium
In the presence of Their Majesties King George V and Queen Mary
Presented by George Black and Val Parnell
Musical Director – Richard Crean

THE PROGRAMME

Sixteen Palladium Girls
Harry Prescott's Seven Hindustans
Tom Payne and Vera Hilliard
George Clarke in 'The New Car'
Julian Rose
De Groot with David Bor and Reginald Kilbey
Gillie Potter
'Dance Time' with the Palladium Girls and Max Wall, Chilton and Thomas, Howell Harger and Naldi, Nervo and Knox
Coram and 'Jerry'
Odali Careno
Toto
Will Hay assisted by Will Hay jun. and H. Gordon Saunders
Gaston Palmer
Jack Payne and his BBC Band

1930

It was the beginning of the Depression, with the Wall Street Crash the year before, but the show at the Palladium was far from being a depressing occasion. A rich galaxy of stars was on the bill, including comedy duo Tom Payne and Vera Hilliard, the eccentric Max Wall and his frog hops, comic Will Hay, clown Toto and the BBC dance band with Jack Payne.

The King could hardly have been more fulsome in his praise: 'The best variety programme we have ever seen'; while *The Performer*'s verdict was: 'a complete and unqualified success'.

Apart from the simple broadcasting of the show, the BBC was also having its own impact on the show – an unlikely success on stage was BBC broadcaster Gillie Potter, with his discourse on a range of subjects. The Queen was seen to be 'literally rocking' with laughter at his amusing talk.

Max Wall

1930

An interesting note about the days when smoking was still allowed in theatres: the presenter, George Black, was reported as saying that it was usually the custom at Royal Variety Performances for the audience not to smoke at the beginning of the evening. Nobody would have dared to light up on such an august occasion if it had not been for the King, who enjoyed a smoke soon after the start!

After the show Mr Harry Marlow, organizer and secretary of the VABF, received the following letter from Lord Cromer, the Lord Chamberlain:

> Dear Mr Marlow,
>
> I must just send you a line to congratulate you on the success of yesterday evening's performance. It really was a most excellent show, and, as you could see from the applause in the house, it was immensely appreciated by the audience.
>
> I hope you are satisfied with the financial results of the evening, about which you will no doubt be letting me hear later.
>
> Yours very truly,
> Cromer.

The Royal Variety Performance this year could have been a big break for an American dance act, the Stone Vernon Four, whose leader readily acknowledged the fact when he told the British press how proud he was to be appearing before the King. Unhappily, his wishes were to be dashed. For, only a matter of hours later, he had to announce to the same pressmen that the foursome was now a threesome and they would not be able to perform. Apparently one of their number had left the country. As the rueful spokesman explained, 'He has taken his passport and, I believe, gone to Austria.'

George Clarke

Coram and 'Jerry'

11 May
London Palladium
In the presence of Their Majesties King George V and Queen Mary
Presented by George Black
Musical Director – Horace Sheldon

THE PROGRAMME

Marie Burke
South China Troupe
Max Miller – 'The Cheeky Chappie'
Teddy Brown
Douglas Wakefield with Billy Nelson, Chuck O'Neil and Fred Louin in *The New Garage*
Gracie Fields
The Twenty-four Mangan Tiller Girls; Twelve Carlton Tiller Girls; Twelve Plaza Tiller Girls with Myron Pearl Company; Jack Stanford, Jane Moore, Billy Revell and J. Sherman Fisher's Sixteen Palladium Girls
Johnson Clark
Rich Hayes
Alexander and Mose (James Carew and Billy Bennett)
Alfred Rode and his Tziganes
Al Trahan with Yukona Cameron
Carr Brothers and Betty

1931

It's hard to imagine a more varied bill than that on offer at the 1931 Royal Variety Performance at the Palladium. One of the stars was one of the all-time comic greats, the self-styled 'Cheeky Chappie' Max Miller. The bill also included singer Gracie Fields, the acrobatic South China Troupe, the Hungarian band – Alfred Rode and his eighteen Tziganes – making their UK début, the comedians James Carew and Billy Bennett, and assorted dancing girls.

The King, just recovered from bronchitis, pronounced himself well pleased with the offerings.

Panic was the order of the day for Alfred Rode and his eighteen Tziganes. They were getting dressed to go on stage when a mathematical genius amongst them realized that there were only fourteen shirts to go round! Luckily, Val Parnell had the presence of mind to tear the shirt off comedian Al Trahan's back, and to take his spare one. George Black gave them the one he had been wearing all day, and the last one needed was donated by the landlord of a nearby public house.

The dexterity and skill of an acrobat from the South China Troupe caused a sensation during the finale. He turned an amazing fifty-six somersaults, one after the other!

To be a successful comedian it helps a great deal to have a droll appearance as well as a good line in gags. Douglas Wakefield (Gracie Fields' brother-in-law) had no problem with regard to that. He miserably recalled his feelings before going on for his Royal Variety Performance, explaining, 'I stood in the wings with my teeth chattering, I hope I was as funny on as I looked off.'

Teddy Brown

Douglas Wakefield ►

1931

30 May
London Palladium
In the presence of Their Majesties King George V and Queen Mary
Presented by George Black
Musical Director – Dick Crean

THE PROGRAMME

Ensemble of Specialities with **Stetson, Christopher and Columbus, The Bells, Levanda and the Nine Diamonds**
Billy Danvers
George Clarke with Madge Aubrey in scenes from *By George*
Bud Flanagan and Chesney Allen
Eugene's Magyar Band
Jack Buchanan
Will Fyffe
Dance Scena with **Errol Addison, Iris Kirkwhite, Flanagan and Allen, Nervo and Knox, Naughton and Gold, J. Sherman Fisher's Palladium Girls** and the **Lawrence Tiller Girls**
G.S. Melvin
Jasper Maskelyne
Cicely Courtneidge
Jack Hylton and his Band
Finale with **Little Doreen, Harry Champion, Vesta Victoria, Fred Russell and Marie Kendall**

1932

Two who were to become doyens of Royal Variety Performances made their début at this year's show at the Palladium – Bud Flanagan and Chesney Allen – and it was from this show that sprang the origins of the Crazy Gang who were to be such favourites on these occasions for years to come.

George Clarke and Madge Aubrey caused great amusement when they appeared on stage – in an Austin Seven car. There were plenty of other acts to savour, too – acrobats Christopher and Columbus, David Arram's Magyar Orchestra and Jack Hylton and his Band.

Afterwards, one commentator remarked, 'Not for some years has Variety in England been able to face the future with such confidence and hopes high as now, and, accordingly, the show proceeded with what seemed like even more than its usual buoyancy and spirit.'

And the King commented: 'A wonderful Variety show and how well thought-out.'

Bud Flanagan made his mark in more than one way in this show when a spur-of-the-moment gesture became part of Royal Performance history. 'Rehearsing the National Anthem,' he recalled, 'we were told to turn half left and face the Royal Box. After the Anthem was sung, I impulsively shouted "Hip-Hip" and the rest of the company of a hundred and fifty shouted "Hurrah" three times.'

This spontaneous outburst was so successful it was kept in the performance on the night and remained a tradition ever after.

However, the night itself was tinged with mild disappointment for Flanagan and Allen, again due to a what might literally be termed a 'time-honoured' feature of 'royal shows'. With the programme running over time, the two young comics were asked to trim their act and come off early. 'Although it was a great disappointment for us to cut,' admitted the deflated Flanagan, 'we had appeared in our first royal show.'

Apparently George V had asked for the show to be finished before eleven o'clock, so that the extra police on duty that night on the way back to the Palace would not have to work overtime.

Naughton and Gold

1932

Flanagan and Allen

1932

Jack Hylton and his Band

Marie Kendall

22 May
London Palladium
In the presence of Their Majesties King George V and Queen Mary
Presented by George Black
Musical Director – George Deacon

THE PROGRAMME

Members of the London Palladium Crazy Gang – including Nervo and Knox, Flanagan and Allen, Eddie Gray, Naughton and Gold, Billy Caryll, Hilda Mundy and Lawrence Barclay – and J. Sherman Fisher's Palladium Girls in 'Portsmouth'
Omar – Spins and Steps
The Crazy Gang – 'I Want a Rest'
Billy Russell – Comedian
Geraldo and his Tango Orchestra, with tango dancers **Gaston and Andrée**
Members of The Crazy Gang – 'Furniture on the Tire System'
The Ganjou Brothers and Juanita Richards, supported by Billy Hendrix, Aline Fournier and Vittorio Togo – 'A Romance in Dresden Porcelain' told in Songs and Steps
Members of The Crazy Gang – 'The Same Romance in Stove Enamel'
Cardini – Britain's foremost Prestidigitator
The Company – ''Apply' Ampstead' sketch
The Carlo Medini Six – Novelty Acrobatics
J. Sherman Fisher's Palladium Girls
The Crazy Gang – 'Fire Drill'
Wilson, Keppel & Betty – Comedy in Dance
William & Joe Mandel – Comedy Trampolinists
Billy Bennett – 'Almost a Gentleman'
Evelyn Laye, Jack Hobbs, Roy Fox and His Band in *Dreams*

1933

Billy Bennett, a great comic star of the day, proved to be one of the main attractions of this show at the Palladium. Billed as 'Almost a gentleman', and celebrated for his eccentric monologues that amounted to oral slapstick parodies of famous compositions like 'Gunga-Din', 'The Road to Mandalay' and 'The Green Eye of the Little Yellow God', Billy Bennett delighted the Royal Box every bit as much as the rest of the audience.

There was plenty of comedy on offer, too, with Flanagan and Allen and Nervo and Knox, and, though somewhat unlikely, the dance team of Wilson, Keppel and Betty was a great comic hit.

The opening to the show was entitled 'Portsmouth' and contained dancing, singing and comedy on a nautical theme – so it wasn't surprising that after the show the former naval officer, now King, announced, 'It has been very funny indeed, a most amusing evening.'

Wilson, Keppel & Betty

1933

Richard Crean, the Palladium's musical director, fell ill only a few days before the performance. His place was taken by George Deacon, the leader of the orchestra.

The King's first words were to enquire about the health of Richard Crean and to wish him a speedy recovery.

During their act, Knox threw a flower at the Duchess of York. Unfortunately, it did not reach its target but landed amongst the decorations surrounding the Royal Box. This did not deter the Duke, who searched until he found the floral buttonhole, eagerly watched by the audience.

Wilson, Keppel and Betty were to become firm favourites with variety audiences for many years. Wilson and Keppel, supposedly a couple of Egyptians, kept everyone vastly amused by their antics while Betty, not to be outdone by her partners, performed an elegant oriental dance that was full of mystery and eastern promise. The act never varied from show to show. Many Bettys came and went – daughter once followed mother in the role! But they drew large houses for year after year.

Today Wilson, Keppel and Betty live on in variety's memory at Brinsworth House in the form of the bar that's named after them.

The skill and consummate ease with which Cardini plucked cards, cigarettes and even billiard balls from the air was greatly admired. It was truly made a 'magical' evening by this master of conjuring!

Geraldo

The Ganjou Brothers and Juanita Richard ►

1933

8 May
London Palladium
In the presence of Their Majesties King George V and Queen Mary
Presented by George Black
Musical Director – Richard Crean

THE PROGRAMME

Kafka, Stanley and Mae Quartette – Aerial Gymnasts
The Three Bonos – New Style Clowns
Frank Boston – Comedy Juggler
J. Sherman Fisher's Palladium Girls
The Three Sailors – Comedy and Dance
Arthur Lucan and Kitty McShane – A Domestic Comedy Episode
Elsie and Doris Waters – Radio Entertainers
Cedric Hardwicke, Osmund Willson and Cicely Oates in *The Carrier Pigeon*
George Robey – 'Prime Minister of Mirth'
The BBC Dance Orchestra directed by **Henry Hall**
Jack Holland and June Hart – Ballroom Dancers with the Lawrence Tiller Girls
Murray and Mooney – Comedians
George Clarke, Bert Platt, Alec Dane and Norah Dwyer in *The Miller's Daughter*
Billy Bennett – 'Almost a Gentleman'
Jack Hylton and his Band

1934

In a year of a Royal marriage – that of the King's youngest son George, Duke of Kent to the lovely Princess Marina of Greece – there was a fittingly rousing Royal Variety show at the Palladium.

The occasion marked the début of the BBC Dance Band conducted by Henry Hall, and saw the 'Prime Minister of Mirth', George Robey, at his peak. An unusual 'act' came when band leader Jack Hylton introduced three top British sportsmen – Fred Perry the tennis player, boxer Jimmy Wilde and footballer Alex James.

The finale saw the Coldstream Guards appearing behind parted curtains at the rear of the stage and they, fittingly, played the National Anthem.

It was the fifth consecutive year that George Black had arranged Royal Performances at the Palladium: 'each performance has seemed to be better than ever' said *The Stage*.

Certainly, the King thought so. 'A wonderful show, better than last year. It gets better every year. The finale was thrilling,' he remarked.

Murray and Mooney

1934

The Three Sailors caused a great deal of mirth by combining their acrobatic skill with high comedy. The farcical misunderstandings only served to create more laughter, though underneath one knew that The Three Sailors had the situation more than adequately under control.

Arthur Lucan and Kitty McShane excelled in a domestic comedy scene in which Lucan played an anxious mother waiting for her daughter, Kitty McShane, to come home. The episode ended with a terrific fight in which every single piece of china on the set was broken.

For Richard Crean, safely restored to the conductor's podium after his indisposition the previous year, the excitement of appearing in a royal show did not diminish. 'I suppose I ought to be used to it by now,' he admitted. 'But every time the drum rolls and the anthem starts . . . a thrill goes right through me!'

The Mills Brothers, featuring as part of Jack Hylton's surprise offering, famed for their prowess at imitating musical instruments, created another 'first' for the Royal Variety Performance when they became the first black artistes to appear in the show.

The visual acts did not translate well over the radio – even with a compère to describe them. This is perhaps the reason why Elsie and Doris Waters were such big hits as their radio characters 'Gert and Daisy'. Popular with their witty definitions – which included the description of golf as 'a game where a ball is chased about by elderly gentlemen who are too old to chase anything else' – they also sang 'Jogging Along' and 'Fed Up' which pleased their radio fans as much as the Palladium audience.

They also proved themselves to be true professionals on the night. Coming on after Old

Arthur Lucan and Kitty McShane

Cedric Hardwicke ►

Elsie and Doris Waters ►

1934

Mother Riley and Kitty had just finished their celebrated crockery-smashing act, Elsie and Doris found themselves obliged to perform against the background noise of broken china being swept up – a task that would have thrown many less accomplished troupers.

Mr George Black, who had by 1934 staged the Royal Variety Performance for a record five consecutive occasions at the Palladium, in that year looked back on the shows: 'One of the striking features,' he wrote, 'has always been the way in which the King and Queen have been quick to appreciate the most homely, domestic jokes.'

The names of artistes to appear were always kept secret until after they had been submitted to Buckingham Palace, and Mr Black said, 'Sometimes attempts to guess the names lead to much heart-burning and disappointment.

'On one occasion a turn whose name had been given in one of these unofficial forecasts actually bought a new stage outfit, only to find, when the real bill was announced, that it was a mistake.'

Rehearsing was always a problem. 'In 1931, when sixty-four girls were included in a dance scene, they were actually rehearsing under the stage while the show was going on.

'After I had seen the performance safely started, I went down into the rehearsal room below the Palladium stage, and there polished the big scene until a few minutes before it was due to go on.'

Mr Black described too how nerves could affect even the most experienced performer before a royal show. 'One comedian a few years ago reached a stage bordering on nervous collapse. He was almost carried to the side of the stage and pushed on.

'He was one of the successes of the evening.

'Then there was a juggler who sat in his dressing room waiting for his call nonchalantly reading a newspaper. At least, so it seemed – until it was noticed that all the time the paper was upside down!'

29 October
London Palladium
In the presence of Their Majesties King George V and Queen Mary
Presented by George Black
Musical Director – Richard Crean

THE PROGRAMME

Hannah Watt, Jeanne Devereaux, Nervo and Knox, Naughton and Gold, Flanagan and Allen, Ernie Gerrard, the Six Lias in 'A Flower Market' from *Round About Regent Street*
The Diamond Brothers – Acrobatic Dancing Comedians
Joe Jackson – 'Silent Comedy'
Stanley Holloway – Monologues
Anton Dolin, Jessie Matthews, J. Sherman Fisher's Palladium Girls in 'A Feathered Flirtation'
The Western Brothers – Entertainers
'Old London Town', excerpts from *Round About Regent Street* with **Jeanne Devereaux, Hannah Watt, Harrison and Fisher, Myles Williams, Flanagan and Allen, The Harmony Revellers, Bea Hutten, Syd Railton, Del Foss, Nervo and Knox, Naughton and Gold**
Boy Foy – England's Youngest Juggler
Sandy Powell with Jimmy Fletcher and Roy Jeffries in 'The Test Match'
Three Cossacks – Roller Skaters
Elsie Carlisle & Sam Browne – Radio Entertainers
Will Mahoney – American Comedian
Arthur Reece, Kate Carney, Gus Elen, Florrie Forde, Harry Champion in 'Cavalcade of Variety', introduced by **Stanley Holloway**
Harry Roy & His Band

1935

Any Royal Variety Performance has a special aura, but the sense of excitement and expectation was even greater than usual in 1935's show, coming as it did in King George and Queen Mary's Silver Jubilee Year. This was in spite of the King's illness, which placed a question mark over the show until his improvement at last confirmed that everything would go ahead as planned.

The show had everything – comedy, dance, song and even roller skating from the Three Cossacks, and so great was the clamour for seats that getting a ticket was a performance in itself. George Black was incredulous at the demand. 'Applications from all parts of the world have been received for seats at next year's show,' he admitted with some amazement. 'If a Royal Variety Performance is held, every seat may be considered sold. Such a thing has never happened before. We could have sold this year's house over and over again. An American millionaire who landed in this country a day or so ago offered £500 for two seats . . . All the cheap seats for this year were sold a year ago.'

In every respect this show formed a fitting climax and, sadly, an appropriate finale to the great encouragement and support that the King had given to the variety profession. For the 1935 Royal Variety Performance proved to be George V's last. The sovereign who, to paraphrase Sir Oswald Stoll's words back in 1912, had invited 'the Cinderella of the arts' to the ball, died a few months later, in January 1936, leaving the royal patronage to live on in his heirs and successors.

Elsie Carlisle

Sam Browne

1935

The night before the Royal Variety Show, the audience at the London Palladium were treated to a sneak preview of the best jokes for the special night! This impromptu 'rehearsal' was to judge the timing of the laughs so that the Royal Performance could be planned to a tight schedule.

The 'Feathered Flirtation' scene, arranged by Ralph Reader, was a wonderful delight for fans of song and dance. The dancing of Anton Dolin was considered superb, greatly complemented by the wonderful voice of Jessie Matthews. The singer was backed by J. Sherman Fisher's Palladium Girls, who were exquisitely dressed in stunning apparel.

An unusual act this year was Boy Foy, a seventeen-year-old juggler who delighted the Palladium audience by performing his tricks while cycling around the stage on a unicycle.

A surprise group of performers drew one of the largest cheers from the audience. They were none other than the residents of Brinsworth House.

Frank Bertram, aged ninety-four, who rang his hand-bells at Osborne for the entertainment of Queen Victoria, had a special introduction, as did Alice Leamar, who sang a verse and chorus of her famous song, 'Her Golden Hair Was Hanging Down Her Back', to prove that she retained her old ability.

Nerves struck Will Mahoney in a truly dramatic way. When he heard the National Anthem at the start of the evening, he became comatose, lying across the xylophone on which he would be dancing later.

Stanley Holloway

Will Mahoney

1935

Jessie Matthews

15 November
London Palladium
In the presence of Their Majesties King George VI and Queen Elizabeth
Presented by George Black
Musical Director – Jack Frere

THE PROGRAMME

Len Lewis, George Lane, Raymond Newell, Henry Carlisle in 'Berkeley Square, Mayfair' from *London Rhapsody*
Norman Evans – Comedian
Florence Desmond – Impressionist
Wences – Ventriloquist
George Formby – Comedian
Cicely Courtneidge with **The Harry Dennis Dance Sextette and The Sherman Fisher Girls**
Max Miller – Comedian
Raymond Newell, Serge Ganjou, Mary Young, Rosarito, George Ganjou, Syd Railton, The Gypsy Boys' Band, The Sherman Fisher Palladium Girls in 'A Gipsy Camp, Epsom Downs' from *London Rhapsody*
Jack La Vier – 'The Man on the Flying Trapeze', assisted by Ruthie Morgan
Ethel Revnell and Gracie West – 'The Long and the Short of It'
Ralph Reader's Gang Show
The London Palladium Crazy Gang in 'In the Shadow of Eros – Piccadilly', from *London Rhapsody*
Gracie Fields – England's Foremost Comedienne
Will Fyffe – Scottish Character Comedian

1937

After a gap, the Royal Variety Performance came back with a flourish two years later, for the 1937 show, once again at the Palladium, and this time before King George VI and Queen Elizabeth, watching their first Royal Variety Show as monarchs.

They were treated to Max Miller at the very height of his comic powers, to Gracie Fields, the Crazy Gang, the brilliant impressionist Florence Desmond, George Formby in his one and only London Royal Variety Show, and Ivor Novello conducting the Palladium orchestra.

This stunning show also coincided with the longest-ever BBC radio broadcast of the performance. It ran from 8.05 pm to 9.30 pm and then from 9.50 pm to 10.50 pm.

Florence Desmond

1937

Most commentators that night agreed that Max Miller, the 'Cheeky Chappie', stopped the show. Perfectly natural and, in the words of *The Times*, displaying 'his usual engaging intimacy with the usual shattering effect upon any gravity that might still be lurking in an odd corner of the house', he was rewarded by the first unconstrained laughs of the evening.

With his legendary sartorial idiosyncrasy, he managed to outshine even his flamboyant wardrobe, appearing in a strikingly patriotic costume of red, white and blue checked coat, pantaloons and shoes. 'I know how to dress for these occasions: nice and quiet!' he confided amid loud laughter in which the King and Queen joined with relish.

A little later in his act he was telling a favourite story about a sailor who returns home, buys a cricket bat, raps on his front door with it and then dashes round to the back. Half-way through, with the audience in convulsions, he stopped, grinned, and said with a sly glance to the Royal Box, 'No, not tonight . . . any other night but not tonight', and then went on to finish one of his sauciest stories just as he always did!

Reported to be a great favourite of the Queen, Will Fyffe was a highlight of the evening, although not without a little help. When he sang 'One Hundred Pipers and a' and a'', one hundred pipers really did come on! They were members of the Greys, the Camerons and the Scots Fusiliers, and were given a standing ovation.

Unknown to the audience, George Formby was paying a special tribute to his father. Under the lapel of his suit, Formby had a diamond and sapphire pin which he wore for luck. It had belonged to his father, George Formby Senior, given to him by George V when he performed at a private party of Lord Derby's in 1913. Formby Senior had worked even when he knew that he was dying so as to provide for his family.

Norman Evans

Ethel Revnell and Gracie West

George Formby

1937

9 November
London Coliseum
In the presence of Their Majesties King George VI and Queen Elizabeth
Presented by George Black
Musical Director – Jack Frere

THE PROGRAMME

The Crastonians
The Two Leslies
Murray and Mooney
Evelyn Laye
Richard Hearne and Rosalind Atkinson in a scene from *Running Riot*
The Stuart Morgan Dancers with Lita D'Oray, Harold Hart and William Kat from *These Foolish Things*
Renée Houston and Donald Stewart
Ken Davidson and Hugh Forgie (badminton display) with Joe Tobin
From *These Foolish Things*, Jack Payne's Orchestra with Peggy Cochrane, Mary Lee, Betty Kent, Biddy Barton, Teddy Foster, Ronnie Grenarder, Rob Ashley
The Dagenham Girl Pipers Three Aberdonians Les Allen
Laurie Day and Roy Willis Will Hatton and Ethel Manners
Elsie and Doris Waters
The John Tiller Girls
Lupino Lane with George Graves, Betty Frankiss, Teddy St Denis with the *Me and My Girl* company
Finale – 'The Lambeth Walk', with 250 artistes, including Jack Barty, George Carney, Clapham and Dwyer, Harry Claff, Harry Champion, Kate Carney, Will Fyffe, Florrie Forde, Gaston and Andrée, Tommy Handley, Lupino Lane, G.S. Melvin, Talbot O'Farrell, Gillie Potter, Harry Tate, Vesta Victoria, Bransby Williams, Anona Winn

1938

No one could have known it at the time, but the 1938 Royal Variety Performance – held at the Coliseum for the first time in ten years – was to be the last until 1945. The finale to the show – involving around 250 artistes – was the biggest ever for a Royal Variety Show and seemed an appropriate if unintentionally grand way to signal the grim and desperate years ahead. Many of the performers were to provide vital work over the next years in boosting the morale of our troops all around the world.

After the show the Lord Chamberlain, Lord Clarendon, sent a letter to the organizer of the VABF Mr Harry Marlow. It said: 'The King and Queen enjoyed the performance very much, and I am asked to convey to Sir Oswald Stoll and yourself, Their Majesties' appreciation of all the excellent arrangements that were made.'

Will Hatton and Ethel Manners

1938

The high point of the show, 'The Lambeth Walk', from the show *Me and My Girl*, was nearly the disaster of the evening. The problem centred on the revolving stage which had taken virtually all day to set up. Lupino Lane was supposed to lead the company into the 'Lambeth Walk'. However, the revolving stage started turning in the opposite direction, threatening to end Lane's performance before it had begun! Luckily, the technical problems were sorted out at the last minute and the number was a great hit.

Who wants to be a producer when you can be in the 'royal show'? Fourteen months prior to the Royal Variety Performance, Gene Gerrard was the producer of *Me and My Girl*, but resigned when there was a 'friendly disagreement' with Lupino Lane. All was forgiven and forgotten, however, for at this year's show, Gerrard was given a walk-on part.

For the screen heart-throb Gary Cooper, who was invited to watch the show from the dress circle, having arrived at the theatre in dark glasses, there was only one star that night – the Queen. 'I am only stopping here a week. I am going to Paris for three days and then racing back to work,' he told reporters before adding, 'It is going to be the greatest thrill of my life to see the triumph the Queen will have in America.'

The 1939 Royal Variety Performance was scheduled to be held at the Palladium on 6 November. However, a couple of weeks following the declaration of war on 3 September of that year, Harry Marlow, the organizing secretary of the then Variety Artistes' Benevolent Fund, was officially informed by the Lord Chamberlain that, in view of the Government's general policy in respect to large numbers of people assembling in a confined space, His Majesty had had no alternative but to cancel the performance.

5 November
London Coliseum
In the presence of Their Majesties King George VI and Queen Elizabeth
Presented by Prince Littler
Musical Directors – Reginald Burston, Van Phillips
Stage Director – Robert Nesbitt

THE PROGRAMME

'Fiesta' from *The Night and the Music* with **Beryl Kaye, Roy Mitchell, Jill Manners**
The Nine Avalons – Skating Act
Duggie Wakefield with Roy Jefferies, Chuck O'Neil, Billie Nelson
Delya – Variety's Lady of Song
Sid Field with Jerry Desmonde, Stella Moya, Denise Clifford in 'Golf'
Jules Adrian and Grace Spero – 'The Musical Act Superb'
Vic Oliver, assisted by Slim Allan
'Bird's-Eye View' from *The Night and the Music* with **Jill Manners, Roy Mitchell, Beryl Kaye**
Maurice Colleano – Variety's Dancing Funster
George Doonan – Comedian
Will Hay with Billy Nicholls, Peter Byrne, Michael Hunt in 'The End of the Term'
Wilson, Keppel and Betty – 'Cleopatra's Nightmare'
Webster Booth and Anne Ziegler – Singers
Tommy Trinder – Comedian
The Combined Stoll Theatres Orchestra with The Coliseum Chorus, Corps de Ballet and Entire Company

1945

This was billed the Victory Royal Variety Performance, coming as it did a matter of months after the end of the Second World War. Inevitably it was an occasion of patriotic celebration. A policeman on duty expressed the general feeling of excitement and wonder: 'Most of the young folks here had no idea that London could put on an event like this. This is really something like peace.'

Two of the 'young folks' present that night were the Princesses Elizabeth and Margaret Rose, who joined the King and Queen at the Coliseum for their first Royal Variety Performance. His Majesty, dressed in naval uniform, and his family were given a rousing reception when they entered the Royal Box.

The Coliseum at this time was staging *The Night and the Music*, an immensely popular show by Robert Nesbitt which ran for some eighteen months. As producer of *The Night and the Music*, Robert Nesbitt also took the 'royal show' under his wing – the first of the twenty-five he was to produce, a record that will perhaps remain unequalled in the history of the Royal Variety Performance. As became the pattern for many subsequent 'royal shows', several big numbers from this resident show were included in the programme, augmented by other artistes. Tommy Trinder was brought in as compère, melding the performance together with his humour, and extracting laughs even when coping with the distracting noise of scenery being moved behind the curtain. 'I don't know where they get the labour from,' he quipped and won a knowing and delighted round from the audience.

There was further comedy from Sid Field, Jerry Desmonde and George Doonan, making their royal début. The American comic, Vic Oliver, was there too, as was Will Hay. In the words of one commentator after the show, 'It has been a reminder that this harassed post-war world can sometimes forget its squabbles in good-humoured laughter and delight.

Sid Field

Maurice Colleano

1945

This was the fourth time Will Hay and his company appeared in a Royal Variety Performance, and included among his assistants in the scholastic comedy routines was actor Peter Byrne, who later achieved widespread popularity as Sgt Andy Crawford in the long-running television series *Dixon of Dock Green*.

One of the biggest successes this year was the Colleano family, Maurice, Rubye, Joyce, Bonar and George, who drew on their circus background to thrill and amaze the Coliseum audience.

A novelty act called The Nine Avalons certainly caused a stir. They were the only speciality act of the night and created a great deal of excitement in the audience with their expert skating and feats of great skill. They seemed to be of particular interest to Princess Elizabeth and Princess Margaret, who were seen whispering to each other and excitedly pointing out the items that pleased them best.

According to some reports, the dress rehearsal for the 1945 show bore all the hallmarks of the classic show business adage 'The worse the dress rehearsal, the better the opening night'. Though, given the very limited time then available to rehearse, hitches with lights, sound and cues were hardly surprising. At one point Jules Adrian and Grace Spero were playing their romantic music when they were plunged into a lurid green light, which did little to cultivate the atmosphere they were seeking.

Sid Field and Jerry Desmonde performed their very popular golfing sketch, considered a classic of variety humour. Field, absurdly dressed in loud golfing trousers, floppy cap and voluminous sweater, was supposed to be receiving his first golf lesson from the altogether more restrained Desmonde. The sketch was a masterpiece of misunderstanding in which the pupil managed to misconstrue just about everything the Pro told

Vic Oliver

Tommy Trinder

him to do, from making a 'tee' of sand, which Field interpreted as the soothing beverage usually associated with the afternoon, to being told to 'skip' an instruction that was evidently beyond him, which had Field jumping over the golf ball to Desmonde's mounting wrath. The audience loved every moment of it.

Will Hay

4 November
London Palladium
In the presence of Their Majesties King George VI and Queen Elizabeth
Presented by Val Parnell
Musical Director – Paul Fenoulhet
Stage Director – Robert Nesbitt

THE PROGRAMME

'Rain and Shine' from *High Time* with **The Girls, Tony Hulley and Barbara Bentham, Brent Fields, Billy Castle and Bobbie Tranter, Mary Naylor** **Cairoli Brothers** – Clowns
Nat Jackley – 'The Raw Recruit' with **Harry Moreny, Dick Beamish, Arthur Vollum and Sammy Curtis**
Bob Bromley and his Puppets **Terry-Thomas** – 'Technical Hitch'
Dance Ensemble with **Alan & Blanche Lund, Gill Johnson, The Three Ross Sisters, Halama and Konarski, The 'Cabana' Accordian Six** **Nat Mills & Bobby** – 'Let's Get On With It'
Robert Lamouret – Ventriloquist **Arthur Askey** – 'I Thank Yew'
'A Yukon Saloon, 1898' with **Harry Lester and his Hayseeds, Tessie O'Shea,** and 'Millionaire Guests' including **Arthur Askey, Charlie Chester, Dick Henderson, Jimmy Jewel, Charlie Naughton, Jimmy Gold, Eddie Gray and Terry-Thomas**
A Pot-Pourri of Speciality Acts: **El Granadas & Peter** – Ropes and Wheels; **Jack Jackie** – Equilibristic; **Koba & Kalee** – Balance; **Reggie Redcliffe** – Xylophone; **René Strange** – Cartoonist; **Henri Vadden** – Juggler
Woodrow – 'Hats Off to Youth' **Sid Field with Jerry Desmonde, Alfie Dean** in 'Billiards'
The Wallabies and the Palladium Boys and Girls
'Shore Leave' with **Jimmy Jewell, Ben Warriss, Marianne Lincoln, Tessie O'Shea** **Three Sailors** – Knockabout Comedians
'Sea Shanties' with **Oscar Natzke** and members from the *High Time* and *Piccadilly Hayride* companies
Band of the Training Ship *Arethusa*

1946

The King and Queen, joined by the two princesses, were treated to a rich array of talent at this year's show at the Palladium.

Comic turns included the irrepressible Arthur Askey, who was warmly applauded by the Royal Party even before he appeared; the comic duo of Jimmy Jewel and Ben Warriss, appearing for the first time at a Royal Variety Show; Sid Field, Terry-Thomas and comedienne Tessie O'Shea.

An unexpected star was twenty-year-old Mary Naylor, the daughter of a taxi driver, whose 'English rose' looks and fine singing captivated the audience.

Left to right: Nat Jackley, Sid Fields, Nat Mills, Arthur Askey and Jimmy Jewel

1946

Police stepped up their presence outside the Palladium after problems handling a large crowd at the Royal Film Show on the previous Friday. Labour MP Tom O'Brien, who was present on that night, said Royal Command Performances should be halted if they were to degenerate into 'hysterical hooliganism for lack of foresight and competence in high places'.

Sid Field came very close to missing his second royal appearance when he was nearly knocked unconscious after his car collided with a van outside Buckingham Palace two days before the show.

Luckily he was well enough to appear, and came on with his superb feed, Jerry Desmonde – this year to have an exasperating game of billiards. Told to 'pocket the ball', a look of complete bewilderment came over Field, until with a smile he put the ball in his trouser pocket and started walking away with a ridiculous grin on his face.

That night he also treated the audience to other memorable comic creations like 'Slasher Green' and 'The Photographer'.

Eddie Gray was not amused when a dastardly souvenir seeker robbed him of his prized possessions. While Eddie was rehearsing for the show, his famous moustache, stage clothes and props were stolen from his car!

Ever since the Royal Variety Show's early days artistes have had a feeling that audiences are perhaps a little more critical or formal than at other variety venues. But big-hearted Arthur Askey wasn't prepared to let that spoil his fun and he immediately warmed his 1946 audience when he looked out into the house and told them, 'All you people in evening dress tonight – like a waiters' convention!'

Tessie O'Shea was a very gutsy performer and well-loved for her sense of humour. As *The Stage* said, 'She seems at her best when almost

Arthur Askey

Terry-Thomas

over-bubbling with comedy . . . her performance was a first-class one. She put over the *Money* number extremely well, and every word was heard throughout the house.'

At Royal Variety Performances, rules are rules and apply to all and sundry, as none other than J. Arthur Rank discovered to his cost in 1946. Rank was expected to be present to say farewell to the Royal entourage after the performance. He was, however, a little slow in leaving his seat after the final curtain and had to stand to attention during the National Anthem. Still hoping to catch the Royal Party, he was stopped and refused admittance by an attendant who said, 'No one can go up these stairs after the Anthem, until the Royal Party has left.'

Tessie O'Shea

Nat Mills & Bobby

3 November
London Palladium
In the presence of Their Majesties King George VI and Queen Elizabeth
Presented by Val Parnell
Musical Director – Paul Fenoulhet
Stage Director – Charles Henry

THE PROGRAMME

'Show Time' with **Hy Hazell, the Alec Thomas Quartet, Marilyn Hightower, Three Shades, Valerie Tandy, Bobbie Tranter, Tony Hulley, The Three Astaires, Hortobagyi Troupe**
Billy Russell – 'On Behalf of the Working Classes' **Wilson, Keppel and Betty** – Sands of the Desert
Norman Evans – Comedian
Borrah Minevitch's Harmonica Rascals, featuring Johnnie Puleo
'All at Sea' with **Mervyn Saunders, Mona and Olivier and The Girls**
Wally Boag – A Lesson in Inflation
'Belle Vue Crescent' from *Together Again* with **Bud Flanagan, Jimmy Nervo and Teddy Knox, Charlie Naughton and Jimmy Gold, Frank Holloway, Willie Carlisle, Freddie Malcolm**
Jack Durant – Impressions
'Among the Heather and Hills' with **Robert Wilson, The Dagenham Girl Pipers, Vic & Joe Crastonian, James Currie's Water Spectacle, Alan Bailey**
Pot Pourri of Speciality acts: **Terri Carol** – Paper Tearing; **Cynthia & Gladys with Indian Clubs; The Three Garcias** – Acrobatic Dancers; **Levanda** – Foot Equilibrist; **Marie Louise** – Aerial Trapezist; **Mariora** – Juggler; **Olga Varona** – High on the Rope; **Eva May Wong** – Charm from China
Bobbie Kimber – Ventriloquist **Dolores Gray & Bill Johnson** – Singers
Laurel and Hardy – Hollywood's Comedy Couple **The Zoris** – Jungle Shadows
Tommy Trinder – 'You Lucky People' **Gracie Fields** – The Lass from Lancashire
Finale – 'There's No Business Like Show Business' with the entire company

1947

Laughter was the main theme of this year's show at the Palladium. For the Royal Party it was already a happy occasion – the Princess Elizabeth appeared in the Royal Box with her fiancé Philip Mountbatten, and the romance of the occasion bestowed a special atmosphere on the evening. And the cast list was virtually guaranteed to produce humour. The famous duo Laurel and Hardy were over from the United States for the show; Tommy Trinder and the Crazy Gang were once more outstanding, and there were acclaimed performances from impressionist Jack Durant and female impersonator and ventriloquist Bobbie Kimber – a man who confused some of the audience as to his real gender.

But 1947 did not lack song either, with Gracie Fields, already a veteran of 'royal shows', getting an exceptionally warm reception.

The King was clearly tickled by the evening. 'We haven't laughed so much for years,' he said later.

Borrah Minevitch's Harmonica Rascals

1947

Despite his acknowledged success with Royal Variety audiences, Tommy Trinder showed that performers can be very superstitious. During a rehearsal, somebody asked if they could photograph the comedian. Tommy immediately refused and ran away, saying, 'The hit of the Royal Variety Show is always a comedian who does not have his picture taken at the dress rehearsal. It was Arthur Askey last year.'

Val Parnell, who presented the 'royal show', later explained the policy of including a few foreign big-name acts at the expense of some home-grown talent. 'We try to show off our variety business to Their Majesties the King and Queen to the best possible advantage.

'We cannot afford in a performance like this, when people are paying ten guineas for a seat, to experiment too much.'

He added: 'The audience at a Royal Variety Performance is hard-boiled and there's nothing worse than for an act to be received in stony silence.

'I don't say that variety is exactly on trial at this show but it is a test performance and obviously, for the sake of the business, we have to put on the very best possible show.'

Billy Russell was a comedian of great skill who did not fear the difficult first spot. His appearance and his make-up of large moustache, the unkempt clothes and his watch chain were more than enough to make his audience roar with laughter.

Irving Berlin's musical *Annie Get Your Gun* was taking London by storm in 1947, and Dolores Gray, star of the show, was invited to appear before Their Majesties. This called for split-second timing on her part. The moment the curtain fell on the evening's performance of *Annie Get Your Gun*, she had to dash from the Coliseum to the Palladium, arriving in the wings just one minute before her cue!

Billy Russell

Bobbie Kimber

1947

After over forty years in show business, Laurel and Hardy made their royal début in 1947 in a piece especially written for the night.

Stan Laurel, a former member of Fred Karno's theatre company who had made the move to America along with Charlie Chaplin, was no stranger to the boards.

Oliver Hardy had started out in theatrical management and played villains in his early films before teaming up with Laurel to form the most famous comedy duo in the world.

Their appearance at the 1947 Royal Variety Show was a high point in the limited variety tour they made of this country – a tour in which they were received with great warmth and enthusiasm wherever they played.

Laurel and Hardy

1 November
London Palladium
In the presence of Their Majesties King George VI and Queen Elizabeth
Presented by Val Parnell
Musical Director – Henry Hall
Stage Director – Charles Henry

THE PROGRAMME

The Blackpool Tower Circusettes 'Up in the Air' with **The Cromwells, Krista & Kristel, The Myrons**
Warren Latona and Sparks – Killing Work **Cheerful Charlie Chester and his Radio Gang**
'Time Out For Dancing' with **Daphne Kiernander and *Skyhigh* Corps de Ballet, Jayne and Adam di Gatano, The Colstons, Nicholas Brothers, The Twenty-Four John Tiller Girls**
Ted Ray – Fiddling and Fooling **George and Bert Bernard** – Off the Record
Stewart McPherson, Compère – 'Thanks for the Memory' with: **Randolph Sutton** – Light Comedian; **Nellie Wallace** – Queen of Comedy; **Billy Danvers** – Always Merry & Bright; **Ella Shields** – 'Burlington Bertie'; **Talbot O'Farrell** – Irish Entertainer; **Gertie Gitana** – The Star Who Never Fails to Shine; **G.H. Elliott** – Minstrel
Ted Heath and His Band – Swing Session **Derek Roy** – Comedian
The Radio Revellers – Desert Island Discs **The Melachrino Strings**
Julie Andrews – Our Youngest Operatic Soprano
The Luton Girls Choir
The Great Alexander Troupe – Acrobats
Arthur Askey – Your Old Playmate
Buster Shaver and his trio of Lilliputians
The Crazy Gang
Danny Kaye
The Skyrockets Orchestra

1948

One of the world's great show-business stars, Danny Kaye, the American comic, dancer and singer, was a feature of this year's show at the Palladium and among other big names were comedian Ted Ray, Arthur Askey and Ted Heath and his band. But in many ways the performance was stolen by a thirteen-year-old girl – the singer Julie Andrews.

She won the hearts of the audience with her own solo spot near the end of the first half. And she rounded the night off with a beautiful rendition of the first verse of the National Anthem, standing on a chair and leading the entire company.

'It was a thrilling finish,' said one critic. The King and Queen's verdict on the show: 'One of the best programmes we have ever seen.'

The 'Thanks for the Memory' Company, left to right: Randolph Sutton, Lily Morris, G H Elliott, Gertie Gitana, Ella Shields, Talbot O'Farrell and Billy Danvers

1948

Charles Henry, from Moss Empires Ltd, described the tension behind the scenes. 'It is,' he said, 'an extraordinary thing how some people react to the importance of such an occasion as the Royal Variety Performance.

'On Monday night, at a crucial moment, as one of the comedians waited to go on the stage, he came to me and told some gags and stories and asked me if he should put them in.

'Another artist, a musician in one of the bands, approached me as I was hastily doing something of importance, handed me a one-pound note, and asked me if I could get him four programmes. I had a lot on my mind at the time and told him so.'

He added: 'It is, of course, a momentous occasion for the artists and nerves play a big part.'

Danny Kaye's success at the Palladium earlier in that year had been little short of meteoric. The critic John Barber had headlined his story on the young New York star 'Kid From Brooklyn Conquers London'. Another in the audience for Kaye's first night recorded that it took 'just ninety-five seconds' for him to establish himself as 'the greatest personal success in the history of English music hall for the last thirty years.'

Every other London critic was in agreement. So was the theatre-going public. And so was the Royal Family who went to see him on more than one occasion.

With adulation like this, it was a foregone conclusion that Danny Kaye would be invited to appear in the 1948 Royal Variety Performance. Expectation was high – perhaps too high – for as many artistes down the years have found, the audience on these occasions is like no other. Danny Kaye either failed to appreciate this, or misjudged it. One way or another, he went down well but with nothing like the stupendous acclaim that everyone had anticipated.

All the same, he had the opportunity to end on a high note, joining Bud Flanagan and Chesney Allen in a chorus of their ever popular 'Underneath the Arches', before the three of them sang 'There's No Business Like Show Business'.

As an indication of the reverence in which the Royal Variety Performance is held in the profession worldwide, the British press reported, the Hollywood film on which Danny Kaye was working at the time had to be halted for ten days while he made the trip to London for the show – at an estimated cost of £12,000.

Danny Kaye

1948

Ted Ray, who appeared on the same bill at the Palladium as Danny Kaye, used to introduce him to the audience each night, and the two of them became great friends. After the show one night Kaye asked if he could borrow one of Ted's pieces of soap, which was still subject to rationing. Ted Ray was happy to oblige but asked to have it back when his friend had washed. On his return to the States, Danny Kaye sent him a whole case of soap.

The press, however, decided that there was some rivalry between the two stars and asked, 'Which is better – Kaye or Ray?'

On the night of the 'royal show' there was little doubt, though Ted Ray – who opened with the line 'I've been in this business forty years and now I'm down to doing a one-night stand' and continued as a storming success – would never have seen himself as 'better' than Danny Kaye.

Following her overwhelming success on the night, Julie Andrews offered her thanks in the pages of *The Stage* in the following announcement:

The Old Meuse,
Walton-on-Thames,
Surrey.

To all my Friends,

Mummy and Daddy join me in a big Thank You for your great help and guidance, and especially dear Madam Stiles-Allen for her patience and loving care during my lessons.

JULIE ANDREWS.

To sound a sadder note, this was the last performance of the comedienne, Nellie Wallace, who collapsed as she came off the stage and died several days later.

Ted Ray ►

Nellie Wallace ►

7 November
London Coliseum
In the presence of Their Majesties King George VI and Queen Elizabeth
Presented by Alec Shanks
Musical Director – Woolf Phillips

THE PROGRAMME

'London Town' **with John Sanger, Arthur Bell, Eric Coates, Phil Parke**
Johnny Lockwood – Comedian
Les Charlivels – International Artistes
Joy Nichols
Michael Bentine – Happy Imbecile
Bill Johnson – The Popular Baritone
Peter Cavanagh – The Voice of them All
'Circus Fantasy' with: **Marilyn Hightower** – Under the Big Top; **Elsa & Waldo** – Grotesque Interlude; **Peggy Ryan and Ray McDonald** – Dancers; **The Tiller Girls** – 'Haute Ecole'
Reg Dixon – Comedian
Band of HM Royal Marines with Frederick Harvey
The Seven Ashtons – Acrobats
Wilfred Pickles
Dolores Gray
Borrah Minevitch's Harmonica Rascals, featuring Johnnie Puleo
Maurice Chevalier
Noele Gordon – 'My Mother's Wedding Day'
Ted Ray – Fiddling and Fooling
Finale – 'Show Business'

1949

The Royal Variety Performances are always popular with the Royal Family, and none more so than this year at the London Coliseum. The King and Queen, accompanied by Princesses Elizabeth and Margaret, rated the show as 'the best ever'. The Queen added that the finale – featuring the HM Royal Marines band and the Sea Cadet Corps – was an 'inspiration'.

The rest of the bill went down well too, notably Noele Gordon (better known later to TV viewers as Meg Richardson in *Crossroads*), who was then starring in *Brigadoon* at His Majesty's, impressionist Peter Cavanagh, and the by-now accomplished Royal performer comic Ted Ray. Another hit, especially with the Princesses, was the youthful Michael Bentine.

Maurice Chevalier

Michael Bentine ►

Wilfred Pickles ►

1949

Michael Bentine's performance took the audience by surprise. For many of them he was an unknown, and it was a little while before this 'happy imbecile' - as the programme described him – got into his stride.

However, by the time he reached his string of impressions – of 'people you've never heard of' – he had them all in stitches and was a big hit with the occupants of the Royal Box. He was, of course, later to be part of the Goons who in turn were much loved by Prince Charles.

Perhaps his own announcement in the next edition of *The Stage* said it all:

Believe me, nobody was more surprised than myself.

Many, many thanks,

MICHAEL BENTINE

SOLE DIRECTION . . . . . MONTAGUE LYON

Ted Ray had been such a success in the previous year's performance that he was asked to appear again and given the top spot, held the year before by Danny Kaye.

Not a performer to be put off by the apparent slowness of his audience, he asked them, 'Will you see the jokes a bit more quickly, please?'

Misfortune can strike anywhere, including the Coliseum stage, as comic Johnny Lockwood found. In making one of his 'falls' midway through his act he hit his nose against the revolving stage. Then, as he sang 'When I go into my Dance', it started to bleed heavily and he had to use his handkerchief to stem the flow. Master comic that he was, he was able to make of it a successful gag, quipping to the delighted audience, 'I was told you wanted blood tonight!'

Afterwards he received a gracious accolade from the Queen, who remarked, 'How plucky of Johnny Lockwood to continue his act as he did.'

Johnny's own comment after the show was, 'I've been falling on stage for fourteen years, and this is the first time I've fallen the wrong way and hurt myself. I said a few things under my breath about the revolving stage.'

Fashion has always been an important factor among both audience and performers: *The Stage* reported that very few ladies favoured the 'new short skirt'. It also reported how Vera Lynn wore pink – and was one of the programme sellers.

The producer Alec Shanks spoke after the show of some of the problems he had to overcome. 'The biggest headache I had on the night was the timing. I don't mean necessarily the split-second signal for the arrival of the Royal Party, but the prompt arrival and just as prompt dispatch of artistes playing other theatres.'

He added: 'I told the artistes on Monday that they needn't worry about the run – it was set.

'That was one thing I tried to do, to get a real homely atmosphere back-stage on the great night – to try to convince the artistes that it was a great night out for them, as much as for the Royal party and the rest of the audience. And in that way I feel that a lot of the nerves associated with such an occasion were overcome.'

Noele Gordon

13 November
London Palladium
In the presence of Their Majesties King George VI and Queen Elizabeth
Presented by Val Parnell
Musical Director – Woolf Phillips
Stage Director – Charles Henry

THE PROGRAMME

'The Warm Up' by **Tommy Trinder**
'Dance Time' from *Out Of This World* with **Sheila Matthews and The Twenty John Tiller Girls, Three Bentley Sisters, The Debonairs, Terry's Juveniles**
Hall, Norman and Ladd
Max Bygraves
Billy Cotton and His Band
Frankie Howerd
'Sing As We Go' **with The Five Smith Brothers, Kaye Ballard, Helen Gallagher, Carole Lynne, Allan Jones, The Merry Macs, Gracie Fields, The George Mitchell Glee Club**
Jonathan Lucas and David Lober with members of the cast from *Touch and Go*
Donald Peers
Jack Benny
Dinah Shore
'Do You Remember?' with **Binnie Hale, Nat Jackley, Naughton and Gold, Max Wall, Nervo and Knox, Max Miller, Flanagan and Allen**
The Band That Jack Built
'Hey Neighbour' with **Bud Flanagan** and the ensemble from *Knights Of Madness*

1950

This was the year of a memorable 'warm-up'. Top comedian Tommy Trinder was given the task of opening the Royal Variety Performance at the Palladium, and attempted the daunting job of cajoling the notoriously unresponsive audience into life.

He was ably assisted in this by the Crazy Gang who appeared in the Royal Box disguised as cleaners and started tossing out discarded programmes and other debris, while light-heartedly threatening parts of the audience with violence if they didn't liven up.

At one point Bud Flanagan dashed into the auditorium, grabbed the young Marquis of Blandford from his aisle seat and ripped out the poor man's starched shirt front. (Little did the astonished audience know that this was actually a paper dickey which the Marquis had willingly agreed to put on earlier in the manager's office.)

To underline the message, Tommy Trinder jokingly introduced the first act, telling the audience, 'Now, you've all been warned – well, perhaps not all of you' as the Royal Party took their seats.

Trinder was one of the hits of the show which also saw Jack Benny the American comic, legendary British comic Max Miller, Max Bygraves and Max Wall. Musical interest was supplied by, among others, Gracie Fields, Billy Cotton and his band and Jack Hylton.

Meanwhile, the first part of the show was given to the theme 'Dance Time', with dancing led by Sheila Matthews, with contributions from the twenty John Tiller Girls and a group called the Debonairs.

Sheila Matthews

1950

As any artiste will confirm, every little detail counts, everything has to be perfect for the big night. The white dress of Dinah Shore was somehow dirtied by the microphone. The stain must have been very small as Val Parnell assured her that it could not be seen from the front seats or the Royal Box – but even so it had to be rushed away to be cleaned. Stage presence and confidence had to be maintained – as Dinah said, 'I know it's there and it spoils it.'

A few days before the show – the 21st Royal Variety Performance – organizers Val Parnell and Harry Marlow threw a party for the artistes (and press) at London's Café de Paris. In his amusing speech, American comic Jack Benny, who had flown all the way from the States for his appearance, recalled that when he stepped off his aeroplane Mr Parnell said to him: 'You have four minutes on Monday, and don't you overdo it'! Benny told the audience he was only concerned about his expenses.

When Mr Parnell spoke, he said he couldn't add to what had previously been said.

'Yes, you can, you can add another six minutes to my time!' interrupted Jack Benny, to laughter all round.

In an extremely candid account of what it feels like to have been less than a rip-roaring success, Frankie Howerd summed up the pain of personal failure on the big night. 'My contribution was not the howling triumph it might have been. In fact, I was a failure . . . I went into my act, but my usual laughs didn't come; I could feel my throat drying up. Emotions crowded in upon me – panic, a determination not to show it, a terrible feeling of loneliness, helplessness, defiance, and Heaven knows what! I kept on talking. I struggled, but apparently they didn't think I was funny, and after a while I became quite certain myself that I wasn't.

Donald Peers

Max Bygraves

1950

'They applauded at the end – how much I have no idea – and I rushed into the dressing-room. As calmly as I could, I sat down and took my make-up off. My hands were trembling – I wanted to crawl into a hole and hide! I did the next best thing. With a hat pulled well down, and coat collar turned up, I walked out of the stage door and moved unrecognized through the still waiting crowds, through to Oxford Street and other streets I do not remember. I cannot describe how terrible I felt; I had let so many people down, including myself.'

In the eyes of many, this year's show will be remembered as the one in which Max Miller deliberately ran over his time.

The problem stemmed indirectly from Jack Benny, who had been allocated longer on stage, not unreasonably as he had travelled all the way from the States where he was a huge box-office draw. Max Miller knew that he was as big a draw on this side of the Atlantic, however, and, abandoning the routine he had gone through in rehearsal, he added several extra gags.

The audience loved it, but, being well over his allotted time, he was straining the accepted protocol of 'royal shows' that timing should be stuck to. Charles Henry was standing in the wings calling, 'Come off, Max.'

When Max eventually did quit the stage, Val Parnell, 'The Guv'nor' of Moss Empires, told him in no uncertain terms, 'You'll never work in one of my theatres again.'

'You're twenty-five thousand pounds too late,' Max is reported to have replied, besides which the impresario had already engaged him to play Nottingham soon afterwards.

Indeed, it was only a comparatively short time before box-office returns and a little reflection on all sides had him reinstated.

Frankie Howerd

Max Miller

29 October
Victoria Palace, London
In the presence of Her Majesty Queen Elizabeth
Presented by Jack Hylton
Musical Director – Freddie Bretherton
Stage Director – Alec Shanks

THE PROGRAMME

'The Warm Up' by **The Gang and 'Monsewer' Eddie Gray**
'Blossom Time in Covent Garden' with **The Cavendish Singers, The John Tiller Girls, Erica Yorke, The Victoria Palace Girls, The Marie De Vere Dancers, Vera Lynn**
Harry Secombe The Wiere Brothers
'Radio Times' with **Stanley Black and the Dance Orchestra, Tony Fayne and David Evans, Richard Murdoch and Kenneth Horne, Arthur English, Sally Ann Howes, Jimmy Edwards**
Florence Desmond – Singer **Norman Evans**
'Dancing Times' with **Alan and Blanche Lund, The Victoria Palace Girls, Pearl Primus and her Company, Hoops – The Boys, Joaquin Perez Fernandez and his Latin-American Company**
'Army and Navy' with **The Mary De Vere Dancers, Johnny Hutch and the Seven Volants, Sam Browne and his Singers, The Keyboard Quintette, Carroll Gibbons, Billy Thorburn, Ivor Moreton and Dave Kaye, Charlie Kunz Patricia Morison**
'The Wedding Breakfast' with **Barbara Bruce, Nervo and Knox, Naughton and Gold, Bud Flanagan**
'Song Serenade' with: **Miklos Gafni; Vera Lynn and Michael Dalton** in 'Carriage and Pair'; The 'Floradora Octette' with **Frances Day, Florence Desmond, Sally Ann Howes, Adelaide Hall, Sylvia Peters, Carole Lynne, Valerie Tandy, Anona Winn; Chesney Allen, Bud Flanagan, Jimmy Gold, Eddie Gray, Teddy Knox, Charlie Naughton, Jimmy Nervo, Richard Murdoch; Gracie Fields; George Mitchell Choir**
Jack Radcliffe Cicely Courtneidge and members of the cast from *Gay's the Word* in 'Vitality'
'The Champ' with **Flanagan and Allen**

1951

This year's show at the Victoria Palace was widely regarded as a big success; 'immensely good' was the Queen's own verdict on the performance.

A notable hit was the youthful Harry Secombe in pre-Goon days with his comic and straight singing, whose performance drew a good response from Princess Margaret. Continuing the relatively new concept of a 'warm-up' act was the Crazy Gang who, among other antics, dressed up as Beefeaters to greet the Royal Party on the stairs.

Other star turns were radio stars Richard Murdoch and Kenneth Horne of 'Much Binding in the Marsh', the country's top woman impressionist Florence Desmond, and singer Carole Lynne, my wife!

1951

The audience was in for a surprise this year when the Royal Party arrived – for, along with the Queen and Princess Margaret were nurses Ruth Beswetherick and Doreen Pearce, who had been nursing George VI through his recent illness. His Majesty was still too ill to attend the Victoria Palace but as the Queen told an inquiring Bud Flanagan: 'He is going on very nicely, thank you.' And when told how sorry everyone was that His Majesty couldn't attend the Queen replied: 'So is he, but he is listening in.'

Richard Murdoch and Kenneth Horne appropriately sang 'We're very sorry someone isn't here today and here's a special message that we'd like the band to play', followed by 'Here's a health unto his Majesty'.

The huge cast-list of three hundred caused problems for the Victoria Palace theatre, which was not big enough to accommodate them all. Frantic preparations were made to house nearly one hundred stars in separate theatres, and fleets of coaches were laid on to ferry artistes forward and back from various venues, some more than a mile away.

The shortage of space in the dressing rooms proved to be of little inconvenience to Richard Murdoch who was able to turn the situation into new gags. On hearing that he would be sharing a room with five others, including Jimmy Edwards, Richard said, 'I've made more room by not bringing my coat-hanger. I can hang my coat on Jimmy's moustache.'

The BBC also gave the surprise announcement that it would broadcast the last part of the show on the radio. Therefore, instead of having one listener (the King was supposed to be tuned into a private broadcast), many millions had the pleasure of hearing the Royal Variety Show.

Richard Murdoch

Jimmy Edwards

1951

Arthur English was the unfortunate victim of pranksters during his turn. On looking for his prompt, he found that things were not as they should have been. 'Half-way through my turn I look at a précis of my jokes sewn to the back of my six-foot tie,' he said afterwards. 'But someone had changed the wording tonight. It flummoxed me for a second.' Who could it have been? Not the Crazy Gang, surely?

Arthur English

3 November
London Palladium
In the presence of Her Majesty Queen Elizabeth II and The Duke of Edinburgh
Presented by Val Parnell
Musical Director – Woolf Phillips
Stage Director – Charles Henry

THE PROGRAMME

'Dance Time' with: **The Victoria Palace John Tiller Girls in** 'Poodle Parade' and 'The Phantom Guard'; **The Three Barbour Brothers** – On Stilts; **Medlock and Marlowe** – Masks and Faces; **Nanci Crompton** – Dancing Star from the USA
Three Monarchs – Harmonicomedians
Tony Hancock – London Laughs
Billy Cotton and His Band
Norman Wisdom – Comedian
Winifred Atwell – Singer
Vic Oliver – 'The Old Vic' Himself
'Song Time' with **Three Beverley Sisters; Deep River Boys** – Harmonists; **Billie Worth, Jeff Warren, Donald Burr** in 'Call Me Madam'; **The Crazy Gang; Gracie Fields with the Ilford Girls Choir and the George Carden Ensemble**
Warren, Latona and Sparks – 'Killing Work' **Rob Murray** – Australia's Comedy Juggler
'In Town Tonight' with **Terry-Thomas, Gerry Brereton, John Ellison, George Cameron, Ted Ray**
Beniamino Gigli – Singer
'Songs that Made the Halls' with **Arthur Askey, Max Bygraves, Zoe Gail, Reg Dixon, Deep River Boys, Pat Kirkwood, Jimmy Edwards, Jack Jackson, Vera Lynn, Jewel and Warriss, Josef Locke, Joy Nichols, Ted Ray, Fred Russell, Maurice Chevalier, Gracie Fields, The Crazy Gang, Ian Wallace, The Band of Her Majesty's Coldstream Guards**

Much was expected of this year's Royal Variety Performance and much attained, coming as it did as the first of Queen Elizabeth II's reign.

'This is the best show of all,' was Her Majesty's verdict on the programme, which included a number of artistes making their royal début, among them the Beverley Sisters, singer Ian Wallace, and zany comedian Norman Wisdom whose hilariously eccentric playing of various musical instruments together with his engaging singing voice made his appearance one of the highlights of the evening. Tony Hancock was a particular hit with the Duke of Edinburgh in his sketch featuring a lieutenant-commander in the Royal Navy.

From overseas came artistes like the American comedian Vic Oliver, Australian juggler Rob Murray, who used to mutter under his breath all through his act, and Nanci Crompton who travelled 3,000 miles from New York to dance at the show for a total of three minutes!

A last minute and unexpected addition to the programme was singer Maurice Chevalier, who was engaged for the summer at the Hippodrome. He was introduced to the delighted audience as 'the idol of the French music hall'.

Winifred Atwell

1952

Bud Flanagan had the dubious honour of warming up the audience at this year's show. He tried to make them less inhibited by the presence of Royalty by saying, 'And don't look up to see if the Queen is laughing first, or you'll get on her blinking nerves.'

One of the warmest rounds of applause was reserved for Gerry Brereton, the ex-commando who was blinded during the war. Having memorized his place on stage during the rehearsal, he was able to walk on stage without assistance to sing 'Here in My Heart'.

In his book *By Royal Command*, Bill Pertwee records the darker side of Tony Hancock's tremendous success that night, which was a sad comment on his own assessment of his brilliant career.

Gerry Brereton

Hancock was sharing a dressing room with several other comedians, including Ted Ray, Jerry Desmonde and Norman Wisdom. Sitting at his dressing table he made up slowly, saying little to his companions but helping himself to a glass of brandy every few minutes.

After watching this for a while, Norman Wisdom, who drank very little himself, suggested to Hancock that he thought he'd had enough and perhaps wouldn't be able to perform if he had any more to drink.

In reply Hancock said he was all right and poured himself another glass.

When his call came he left the others in the dressing room anxiously waiting for the tannoy to relay his act from the stage, apprehensive that this time Hancock wouldn't be able to exercise his usual genius.

Their worries were unfounded. Tony Hancock left the stage to thunderous applause and returned to be greeted by his jubilant friends. However, he seemed unmoved by their congratulations, finished off the bottle of brandy, put on

Norman Wisdom

his coat and slipped out of the theatre to find a pub while he waited for the finale.

The much-loved Gracie Fields was appearing in her seventh Royal Variety Performance (her first, astonishingly, was in 1928) and was never more popular with the audience – and the critics. One wrote of her 'charm of personality, glittering technique and appeal of warmth and human feeling'; though the same critic missed the Rochdale-born singer's 'robust fun' and 'honest-to-goodness vulgarity' which marked her earlier years.

In the show she and Gigli came on together to sing their first duet, 'Come Back to Sorrento'. Both were extremely nervous, particularly 'Our Gracie', who confessed before the show, 'I've got butterflies in my stomach – I feel this is all wrong.'

Her worries were soon allayed by the rousing reception she and Gigli received and, boosted by this, the audience heard her sing in faultless Italian. They were also highly amused by her blouse, which was adorned with an image of the Bay of Naples.

On the same bill was another female performer of almost legendary fame – Vera (now Dame Vera) Lynn. After a quiet spell following her wartime fame, Miss Lynn had recently broken into the West End bigtime in shows at the Palladium and the Adelphi.

Vera Lynn

The Deep River Boys

2 November
London Coliseum
In the presence of Her Majesty Queen Elizabeth II and The Duke of Edinburgh
Presented by Prince Littler
Musical Director – Philip Green
Stage Director – Tommy Hayes

THE PROGRAMME

'Musical Memories' with **Peter Knight's Merrymakers, Harry Dawson, Jean Campbell, Pearl Carr, Dick James**

'It's a Grand Night for Singing' with: **Mackenzie Reid and Dorothy** – Scottish Accordionists; **Lizbeth Webb** – In Song; **Alfred Marks** – Comedian; **Edmund Hockridge** – Baritone

Tommy Cooper – Crazy Conjuring

Eve Boswell – The Sugar Bush Girl **Jack Warner**

'Sit Down, You're Rockin' the Boat' – **Stubby Kaye with members of the cast of** *Guys and Dolls*

Jo, Jac and Joni – Burlesque Comedy

Anne Shelton – Singer

Max Bygraves – Comedian

'Dance Time in London' with: **Sheila O'Neill and Veit Bethke** and company in the 'Pony Ballet' from *Paint Your Wagon*; **Danya and Alvarez** – Speciality Dancers; Ice Ballet with **Gloria Nord, Len Liggett and Pam Murray** with members from the **Corps de Ballet** and **The Empire Pool Festival Choir**

The John Tiller Girls

Ethel Revnell – Comedienne **Henry Cotton**

Jimmy James – Comedian **Ronnie Ronalde** – The Popular Favourite

Vivian Blaine from *Guys and Dolls*

Jimmy Edwards – Comedian

Grand Finale with Eamonn Andrews and Entire Company

1953

Her Majesty the Queen, the Duke of Edinburgh and Princess Margaret attended the Coronation Year Royal Variety Performance at the Coliseum – the Duke wearing horn-rimmed glasses for the first time in public. Invited to offer a professional opinion for the reason, a leading London oculist suggested, 'It seems likely that the Duke may be suffering from a very common complaint – slightly short sight.'

The immensely successful production of *Guys and Dolls* was playing at the Coliseum at the time and several numbers were included in the programme for the 'royal show'. However, the careful monitoring given to every item in a royal programme resulted in some delicate changes to aspects of *Guys and Dolls*, which it was felt might possibly cause offence in some religious quarters.

As Harry Marlow, secretary of the Variety Artistes' Benevolent Fund, explained, 'These performances attract people of all religions, and we do not want anything to offend.'

Thus, the Salvation Army uniforms in the show were changed on the night to skirts and blouses, the words 'Save-a-Soul Mission' were discreetly dropped and several other minor amendments were made.

The composer Frank Loesser, was slightly puzzled by the somewhat bizarre permutations. 'There seem to have been some strange cuts,' he commented. 'While the word "heaven" has been changed to "judgement", apparently the phrase "heavenly trip" is permissible.'

Over the years several commentators have observed that performances at Royal Variety Shows have perhaps lacked the uninhibited display seen by other audiences. If this is true, it merely reflects the very great care taken by the producers to ensure that nothing is admitted that could possibly be misconstrued. Perhaps Bud Flanagan expressed this understanding of the special status of the Royal Variety Performance most succinctly when he said after one show, 'Protocol must be observed, and everyone on and off the stage must respect it. Whatever some stars may think of themselves, at a Royal Show the top of the bill is the Monarch, and we the artistes have the privilege of performing in support.'

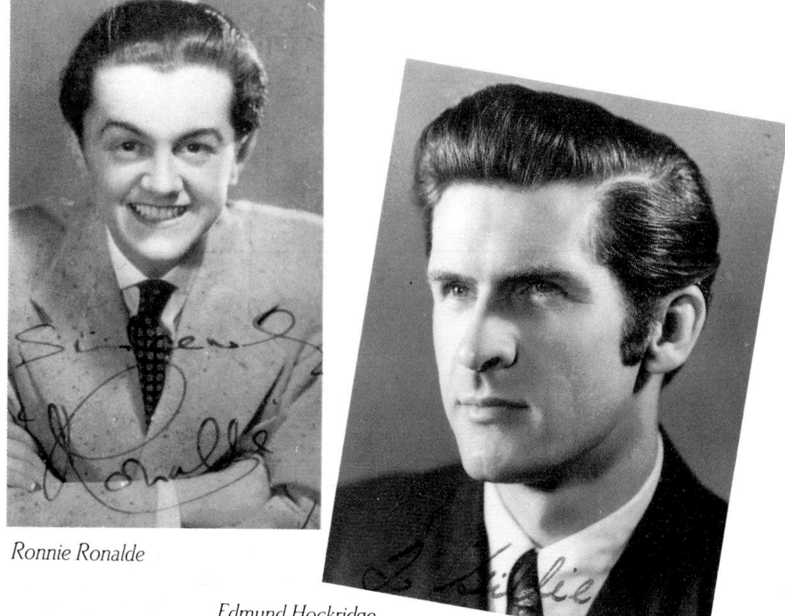

Ronnie Ronalde

Edmund Hockridge

Jack Warner ►

Anne Shelton ►

1953

One of the most accomplished acts of the evening was that of Max Bygraves. *The Stage* said of him: 'Among the newcomers to variety, outstanding is Max Bygraves, who was unknown less than ten years ago.

'He has his own sense of comedy, which he is able to communicate in an individual way. He combines the stuff of music hall, everyday realities and a tinge of romance (which is usually sent sky-high with the flick of a hand or the turn of a lip), with a modern touch and a polish equal to that of any artiste on the variety stage today, here or in America.'

Donald Bamfort and Cynthia Brahms, two of the large Australian contingent in the finale, produced an act that turned out to be practical as well as unusual. The couple, better known as Kenneth and Kathy Kanga, famous Australian comic characters, were at the dress rehearsal in their full-length kangaroo suits, and having found no seats available, came up with the pragmatic solution of sitting on their sturdy tails!

For comedian Jimmy Edwards this was his third Royal Variety Performance in three years. He took the opportunity afterwards to reflect on the problems of appearing in such shows. 'It is a great worry and something of a risk,' he said. 'And sometimes I wonder what it is all about. You cannot help wondering if you can possibly succeed with this very difficult and unrepresentative audience.

'No doubt there are lots of people out there who like variety and want to enjoy the show, but many have come simply because it is a Royal event.

'In my opinion a Royal variety audience is extremely hard to please, one of the most difficult things being to adjust your act to the special atmosphere and relatively small amount of playing time.

1953

'One step wrong at the start and you may be a flop. That has happened ... the Press is eager to report all about the glamour and success of the evening, but it is also ready to pounce on failure.'

He added: 'It is extremely risky to change your act and probably fatal to introduce new material. Better to stick to what you have been doing for a long time and know inside out.'

There was a memorable finale to this year's performance. With the Queen and the Duke of Edinburgh due to set off shortly on a tour of the Commonwealth, the stage was filled with people from member countries all over the world.

They included Australian tennis players and cricketers, surf lifesavers in Bondi Club costumes, Maoris, servicemen and civilians from New Zealand, Fiji, Tonga and Bermuda.

Alfred Marks

Eamonn Andrews

1 November
London Palladium
In the presence of Her Majesty Queen Elizabeth II and The Duke of Edinburgh
Presented by Val Parnell
Musical Director – Eric Rogers
Stage Director – Charles Henry

THE PROGRAMME

'Sawdust and Spangles' from the Palladium Show with **Fay Lenore and the Palladium Boys and Girls**
The Schaller Brothers – Trampolinists **George Mitchell Choir**
Jimmy Wheeler – Comedian
'Music For You' with: **Eric Robinson, his Orchestra and Singers; Eddie Calvert** – with the Golden Trumpet; **Joan Turner** – Singing Comedienne; **Richard Hearne** – Mr Pastry; **Howard Keel** – MGM Singing Star
'The Four Drinkspots' – Chesney Allen, Arthur Askey, Max Bygraves, Bud Flanagan, with Billy Russell, Donald B. Stuart, Brian Reece, Harry Green, Catherine Boyle, and Jack Hylton at the piano
Al Read – 'Right Monkey'
'Romance in Town' **with Norman Wisdom, Gillian Moran, Herbert Hare, Florence & Frederic**
The Crazy Gang with Pat Cutts and Shirley Eaton
'Record Rendezvous' **with Max Bygraves, David Whitfield, Guy Mitchell, Dickie Valentine, Frankie Laine, Jack Parnell and his Orchestra, Ted Heath and his Music, Dawn White and her Glamazons**
The John Tiller Girls Rudy Horn – Juggler
Noël Coward
The Shopgirl Princess, a musical comedy with **Diana Churchill, Jack Buchanan, Joan Sims, Frankie Howerd, Gladys Cooper, Binnie Hale, Peter Sellers, Donald Wolfit, Elsie Randolph, Thora Hird, Leslie Henson, Dick Bentley, Michael Denison, Nigel Patrick, Thorley Walters, Anthony Steel, Brian Reece, Walter Crisham, Bruce Trent, Peggy Cummins, Shirley Eaton, Dulcie Gray, Shani Wallis**
Bob Hope with **Moira Lister, Jerry Desmonde** and **The Hope Repertory Company**

1954

For the 25th Royal Variety Performance, the Jubilee Show, one of the all-time show business greats topped the bill at the Palladium – Bob Hope.

He was one of the fifteen artistes introduced to the Queen after the show. The others were hardly less famous names – Noël Coward, Norman Wisdom and Max Bygraves were just some.

Once again the Crazy Gang warmed up the audience, who had given the Queen a rousing reception. Even so, as *The Performer* reported, 'The stuffed-shirt atmosphere was dispelled only spasmodically as the audience realized they might just as well enjoy themselves.'

Noël Coward

1954

As part of the warm-up, the Crazy Gang sold ice cream and walked in and out of the Royal Box dressed as cleaners – the first time any artiste had used the Royal Box in this way.

As one commentator put it: 'All this got the usually stuffed-shirted audience loosened up before the Queen, looking radiant in white with a dazzling diamond tiara, entered the Royal Box, followed by Princess Margaret and Prince Philip.'

Bob Hope appeared solo and in a sketch with two other big names on the bill, Noël Coward and Jimmy Edwards. But despite his popularity with the Royal Party, he was not without his critics. One said, 'His offering was loosely thrown together and might have been far more telling if it had been more compact.'

Even for performers known for their sophistication and urbanity, the Royal Performance can be a terror on the nerves. Jack Buchanan attributed this in part to the well-to-do audience: 'You can see them sitting there dressed up to the nines, saying, "We've paid twenty guineas a head for our seats so amuse us if you can." '

In the event, the audience and the critics alike were full of praise for him. *The Times* had this to say: 'For charm there was Jack Buchanan, aged sixty-three, impersonating a dapper World War One officer . . . and there was no actor on stage with half his sparkle.'

This year's performance underlined the rich comic talent that was around in Britain at the time: Norman Wisdom, Peter Sellers, Max Bygraves and Frankie Howerd were all in the show. All four were making their names through the newer mediums of radio and television, but, as *The Stage* commented, 'They are already a part of the great tradition of versatile comedy and personal popularity that has made this form of entertainment [variety] unique, and so often honoured by Royal patronage.'

Jimmy Wheeler

Richard Hearne

1954

Prince Philip exchanged notes with singer Dickie Valentine on the state of married bliss. On asking the whereabouts of Valentine's wife of one week, Betty Flynn, an ice skater by profession, the crooner replied that she was in the audience. 'What a way to spend a honeymoon,' said the Prince.

One of the features of the Royal Variety Performance each year are the elegant and fashionable dresses worn by many of the ladies present. But this year the men were also singled out by commentators – notably clothes designer Hardy Amies for the velvet collar of his 'impeccable' tails.

The year marked a remarkable landmark for the organizer of the Royal Variety Show, Harry Marlow. This year's offering raised around £18,000 for the VABF – bringing the total the seventy-year-old fund secretary had raised for the charity to more than half a million pounds.

There was a surprise finale to the show when from all parts of the auditorium came hoards of 'bobby-soxer' girls to mob the singers on the stage, screaming as they went.

Joan Turner

Dickie Valentine

13 April
The Opera House, Blackpool
In the presence of Her Majesty Queen Elizabeth II and The Duke of Edinburgh
Presented by Jack Hylton
Musical Directors – Billy Ternent and Ronnie Munro
Stage Director – Charles Henry

THE PROGRAMME

'The Show Train Comes to Town' with **Lauri Lupino Lane, George Truzzi, Peter Glaze, Kenneth Sandforth, Pamela Bromley, Vera Day, The John Tiller Girls, The Victoria Palace Girls and Boys, Kathryn Moore, The Flying De Pauls, The Barbour Brothers and Jean, The Amandis**
'Be Your Age' **with The Crazy Gang, Morecambe and Wise, Bill Waddington**
'Nothing Less Than Orchids' with **Josephine Anne, The Showgirls, The John Tiller Girls**
Arthur Askey
'Radio Times' with **Geraldo and his Orchestra, Jewel and Warriss, Littlewood's Girls Choir, Joan Regan, Five Smith Brothers, Alma Cogan**
George Formby
'Dancing Times' with: **The Crazy Gang** in 'Frères Jacques'; **1st Battalion The Liverpool Scottish (TA)**; **Beryl Grey with John Field** – Pas de Deux from *The Sleeping Beauty*; **Jack Tripp with The John Tiller Girls; Children from The Blackpool Tower Ballet**
Charlie Cairoli with Paul
Wilfred and Mabel – Ask Pickles
Albert Modley
Lauri Lupino Lane and George Truzzi
Flanagan and Allen
Eddie Fisher with the BBC Northern Variety Orchestra
Al Read

1955

The first of the two Royal Variety Performances of 1955 – and the first ever staged outside the capital – featured many acts familiar to Blackpool audiences. The organist Reginald Dixon who had become a popular resident in the Tower Ballroom was there, with the signature tune he made all his own, 'I Do Like to be Beside the Seaside'. Jimmy Jewel and Ben Warriss delighted their fans as usual. From the Tower Circus came the musical clowns Charlie Cairoli and Paul, while George Formby and the American star Eddie Fisher added to the star-studded line-up, along with Arthur Askey and a couple of young comedians by the name of Morecambe and Wise.

The highlight splapstick act of the evening belonged to the consummate comedians, Lauri Lupino Lane and George Truzzi, who treated the Blackpool audience to their celebrated paper-hanging routine. This was centred round two people trying to paste a piece of wall-paper on a wall with different coloured paste. The consequences can be imagined, and at the end of it both comics had to have a good wash-down before next appearing on stage.

The Cairoli Brothers

Morecambe and Wise

Reginald Dixon

7 November
Victoria Palace, London
In the presence of Her Majesty the Queen and The Duke of Edinburgh
Presented by Jack Hylton
Musical Directors – Billy Ternent and Ronnie Munro
Stage Director – Charles Henry

THE PROGRAMME

Scene from *Jokers Wild* introduced by Tommy Trinder, with Latona, Graham and Chadel, The Victoria Palace Boys and Girls
Dave King Darvas and Julia
Channing Pollock
The Crazy Gang Ruby Murray
Benny Hill with Olivia Dale, Jeremy Hawk, and Ronnie Brodie
Pat Kirkwood with Robert Beatty, Douglas Byng, George Carden, Walter Crisham, John Gregson, Bobby Howes, Hugh McDermott, Terence Morgan, and Brian Reece
Cyril Stapleton with the BBC Showband and The Stargazers
Lena Horne
Scene from *Salad Days* with John Warner, Eleanor Drew, Dorothy Reynolds, Newton Blick, Yvonne Coulette, James Cairncross, Michael Meacham, Christine Finn, Michael Aldridge, Pat Heywood, Joe Greig, and Bob Harris
Johnnie Ray
Scene from *La Plume de ma Tante* with Robert Dhéry, Jacques Legras, Colette Brosset, Christian Duvalein, Pierre Olaf and Company Alfred Drake George Jessell
Scene from *Kismet* with Doretta Morrow and Company
'Judge for Yourself' with Leslie Henson, Jimmy Edwards, Richard Attenborough, Diana Dors, Edmund Willard, Brian Reece, Bruce Seton, Emrys Jones and Lauri Lupino Lane
The Chinese Classical Theatre Company Moscow State Folk Dance Company

1955

The 1955 London audience saw Benny Hill, Lena Horne and an unusual act in the form of the Chinese Classical Theatre Company, along with established favourite Jimmy Edwards. Newcomers included the heart-throb Johnnie Ray and the young Dave King, who had shot to fame on BBC television the year before.

This year also marked the arrival of Independent Television, who made a bid to televise the Royal Variety Show. This was turned down by the Lord Chamberlain's office on the grounds that similar applications by the BBC in the past had met with the same response from the Variety Artistes' Benevolent Fund, who felt at the time that television might endanger variety theatres all over the country.

What a difference thirty years can make in reshaping attitudes!

Johnnie Ray's presence in the cast was greeted with great anticipation. The opening night of his Palladium season had been a sensation with the crowd of adoring fans almost in hysterics as they thronged Argyll Street and the stage door, screaming and banging their fists on the pavement. In the words of Bill Pertwee, who witnessed the amazing scenes, 'I believe it was the first uninhibited fan adulation that this country had experienced.'

For his act Jimmy Edwards chose the popular sketch 'Judge for Yourself' in which he played a bewigged denizen on the bench, which proved once and for all that the law, in the right circumstances, really could be an ass. True to his hilarious buffoonery he asked a wretched defendant how he pleaded and in response to the man's complete breakdown in the dock, Judge Edwards intoned, 'Oh you miserable pleader.'

Ruby Murray

Benny Hill

1955

Lena Horne

1956

Perhaps it was just as well that 1955 had two Royal Variety Performances, for the 1956 one has gone down in the history as the show that never was.

After the months of careful planning, the painstaking vetting of acts and the gruelling demands of bringing together all the disparate elements in less than forty-eight hours before its start, the unimaginable happened and the show was cancelled within four hours of curtain-up.

The cause lay far away in the Middle East, on the banks of the Suez Canal where British troops had landed that morning in Port Said, following previous operations in the past few days against military targets in Egypt. The Soviet Union was threatening to retaliate with rockets unless the British and French forces accepted a ceasefire and, as Val Parnell told a stunned cast as they were finishing their rehearsals, Her Majesty felt unable to attend in the mounting international crisis.

There was widespread disappointment among the cast. The Crazy Gang had specially put together a burlesque of *A Midsummer Night's Dream*. Laurence Olivier, Vivien Leigh and John Mills were on the bill. And Liberace had spent nine days travelling to London for the show – first overland from Los Angeles to New York and then by ship to Southampton. He felt the disappointment keenly and wept openly.

Gracie Fields did what she could to comfort others in the cast as deeply affected, but it was the Cockney comedian Jimmy Wheeler who restored flagging spirits when he took out his violin and announced to a packed dressing room, 'I've rehearsed this bloody act for a fortnight so somebody's gonna hear it' and promptly went into his full routine, adding several gags that would never have found their way into the show proper!

18 November
London Palladium
In the presence of Her Majesty Queen Elizabeth II and The Duke of Edinburgh
Presented by Val Parnell
Musical Director – Cyril Ornadel
Stage Director – Charles Henry

THE PROGRAMME

'The Party's On' from *We're Having a Ball* with **The Kaye Sisters, Max Bygraves, The George Carden Dancers and The George Mitchell Singers**
Bob Monkhouse – The Compère
The Goofers Jimmy Logan
Harry Secombe with The Morriston Orpheus Choir
The Crazy Gang in a scene from *These Foolish Kings*
Leo De Lyon
Gracie Fields
Dickie Henderson
Count Basie and his Orchestra Ralph Reader and his Gang Show
Max Bygraves with Joan Regan and The Kaye Sisters
Judy Garland with Jimmy Brooks
'The Diplomats' with **Bud Flanagan, Bed Lyon, Jerry Desmonde, Alfred Marks, Brian Reece**
Mario Lanza
'Variety': 'Minstrels' with **Norrie Paramor's Big Ben Banjo Band;** 'Ragtime Octette' with **Ronnie Hilton, Dickie Valentine, Malcolm Vaughan, Teddy Johnson, Dennis Lotis, Frankie Vaughan, David Whitfield and Herschel Henlere** at the piano; 'Revue' with **Arthur Askey and Vera Lynn;** Ballet with **Markova; Alma Cogan;** 'Dance' with **The John Tiller Girls;** 'Magic' with **Tommy Cooper;** 'Records' with **Winifred Atwell;** 'Skiffle' with **Tommy Steele and his Steelmen**

1957

The 1957 Royal Variety Performance at the Palladium was evidence of the great range of artistes and experience that the world of show business could draw on in a single night. Topping the bill was the American star singer Mario Lanza, and there were 'veterans' Vera Lynn, Arthur Askey, and the Crazy Gang too. But the show also featured up and coming talent, with Bob Monkhouse as compére, Tommy Steele and his Steelmen and the young Dickie Henderson. One of the newcomers, Scottish comic Jimmy Logan, suffered somewhat from the tension as he admitted afterwards. 'I was nervous. I went on and did my act, got off and was thankful.'

Winifred Atwell

1957

Judy Garland

1957

The year 1957 marked a particular milestone in the education of the young Prince Charles, for that autumn term he began his time at Cheam School, the first heir to the throne ever to attend a boarding school. This was an event that the Crazy Gang could not allow to pass unnoticed and when the Royal Party arrived at the London Palladium that night Her Majesty was greeted by the Gang attired as the headmaster and pupils of Cheam, complete with shorts and blazers.

Photographs in the papers the following day recorded the Queen's uninhibited amusement at the spectacle. However, the BBC chose not to include the Cheam greeting in their coverage. A week after the show a spokesman explained, 'It is not a ban. But the item was not strictly part of the show.'

Dickie Henderson carried on a family tradition by appearing in this show thirty-one years after his father, the comedian Dick Henderson, who played at the Royal Variety Performance in 1926.

The other celebrated event in this year's show revolved around top of the bill, Mario Lanza, who was appearing by arrangement with my brothers Lew and Leslie Grade. Working for them at the time was a young agent named Peter Prichard, who thirty years on is not only one of the leading agents in the profession today, but also the highly influential Treasurer of the Entertainment Artistes' Benevolent Fund. Back in 1957, however, Peter was entrusted by the agency with looking after stars like Mario Lanza.

Arriving at the Dorchester, where they were booked in for the weekend, Peter Prichard was detailed not to let his charge out of his sight, since Mario Lanza was very on edge at the prospect of appearing before a live audience on stage.

To make him feel more comfortable, arrangements were made so that he could rehearse at the Palladium alone with the orchestra. The other artistes were asked to remain in their dressing rooms, and the theatre was cleared of all but a skeleton staff. Indeed, Peter made every effort to ensure Mario Lanza the privacy he had asked for. What he hadn't bargained for was a photographer who suddenly appeared in the dressing room and began to take pictures.

This was too much for the already highly-wrought star and his long-suffering agent was rewarded with a punch on the nose. Justifiably aggrieved at this, Peter nevertheless assented to Val Parnell's entreaty to stick with the temperamental Mr Lanza and not to mention the incident to anyone until after the show the following day.

However, word must have slipped out from some other source, and in an attempt to confirm what had happened, the press rang Peter's home, where his grandmother, who knew nothing of what had happened at the Palladium, took the call. In one of the most memorable quotes in the long history of the Royal Variety Performance, she answered the question as to whether Peter had been in a fight with the comment, 'Oh, very likely, he's always getting into trouble with the kids around here.'

Her grandson's response to being cited as still a 'kid' has not been recorded!

Not that that was the last from Mario Lanza. As he was being presented to Her Majesty the Queen and the Duke of Edinburgh after the show, His Royal Highness remarked pleasantly, 'I hear you are on a European tour at the moment; I hope it's proving successful.'

'If you call five thousand dollars a night successful, yes', replied the star, adding, 'and what's your story?'

With a perfect parry Prince Philip replied, 'Oh my story is about as interesting as my voice,' and continued down the presentation line.

3 November
London Coliseum
In the presence of Her Majesty Queen Elizabeth II and The Duke of Edinburgh
Presented by Bernard Delfont
Musical Director – Harold Collins
Stage Director – Robert Nesbitt

THE PROGRAMME

'Night of Nights' with the *Talk Of The Town* Girls and Boys, The Stargazers, Yana
Max Bygraves – The Compère
'Brothers and Sisters (Real) of Variety' with The King Brothers, The Mudlarks, The Beverley Sisters, The Charlivels Tony Hancock Cyril Stapleton and his Showband
Frankie Vaughan Bruce Forsyth Bernard Bresslaw
Antonio and his Spanish Ballet Company
Roy Castle
'The Good Old Days' from *Large as Life* with Harry Secombe, Harry Worth, Lynette Ray, Hattie Jacques, Max Russell, G.H. Elliott, Hetty King, The George Carden Dancers, The George Mitchell Singers and the Ford Motor Works Military Band
'Dancing Time' with The George Carden Dancers, The Dior Dancers, Victor Silvester and his Ballroom Orchestra, The Mecca Formation Dancers
David Nixon Charlie Drake
Pat Boone – A Visitor From America
Mantovani and his New Music with Harry Secombe and Adele Leigh
Ron Parry Eartha Kitt Kenneth More with Max Bygraves
'Songs from the Shows': Norman Wisdom, Jerry Desmonde, Pip Hinton, Marion Grimaldi, Pamela Gale, Felix Felton, Terence Cooper and members from the cast of *Where's Charley?*; June Bronhill, Thomas Round and members from the cast of *The Merry Widow*; Rex Harrison, Julie Andrews, Stanley Holloway and members of the cast from *My Fair Lady*

1958

The Royal Variety Performance 1958 marked the first of the long-running series of Delfont/Nesbitt productions and began the partnership that year at the Coliseum with a large and impressive cast.

With shows like *Where's Charlie?* at the Palace Theatre, *My Fair Lady* at Drury Lane and *The Merry Widow* at Sadler's Wells there was no shortage of first-rate material to draw on for the Royal Variety Show – and thanks to the revolving stage at the Coliseum it was possible to include a wide-ranging and impressive selection of numbers in the programme.

1958 also marked the highly successful royal début of Roy Castle, who was later to become such a big star of both stage and screen. 'He held the audience in the palm of his hand,' said one glowing notice the following day.

Under the polished compèring of Max Bygraves – a firm Royal Variety favourite by now – there was plenty of other talent to draw on, including Tony Hancock who appeared as a budgerigar in a cage above the stage! He was joined in the act by the much-loved Hattie Jacques playing the bird's owner.

The finale was truly spectacular, with Rex Harrison, Julie Andrews and Stanley Holloway singing songs from *My Fair Lady* and ending with 'I Could Have Danced All Night' accompanied by no less than three orchestras on stage conducted by Mantovani, Victor Silvester and Cyril Stapleton, with yet another orchestra in the pit.

Stanley Holloway

Frankie Vaughan

1958

An example of the careful scrutiny applied to material for any Royal Variety Show came from Norman Wisdom's rehearsal at the end of which he exited doing an eccentric dance step with the line 'I'm trucking off'.

That was no sooner spoken than struck from the act on the grounds that it 'might be misheard'.

Bernard Bresslaw had a few uneasy moments with the protocol of the evening as well. A week before the show, he was told that he had been selected to be 'presented' after the performance and would be expected to appear in tails. Now Bernard didn't possess a tail suit at the time and, standing the best part of six-foot-five, he wasn't well placed to borrow one. The only option he had was to have one made, and the court tailors Kilgour and French agreed to have one ready for him in time.

Roy Castle

They were as good as their word, but come the night Bernard was told that he was going to be presented in his stage costume after all, and his magnificent new tails were denied their royal début.

The inhibitions of the audience were nearly Tommy Steele's downfall. His surprise performance was almost literally a case of 'Singing the Blues' after his request to clap along met with a very poor response. Luckily, the Queen came to his aid, clapping enthusiastically and leading the rest of the house who promptly joined in.

Forty-six years after Vesta Tilley reputedly had Queen Mary retreating behind her programme, Hetty King, another male impersonator, was nearly changed at the last minute for fear of being a shade too outré. In the end the seventy-year-old artiste's act was allowed to remain intact. Dressed as a sailor and winking wickedly, she delighted the audience with her rendition of 'All the Nice Girls Love a Sailor'.

Hetty King

1958

Anxious not to cause provocation by her distinctive way of singing, Eartha Kitt said before the show, 'I sure hope this performance goes all right. The last time I played before royalty – the King and Queen of Greece in Los Angeles in 1953 – I was nearly thrown out of the city. The mayor said I was too wicked. He said I was un-American.'

Eartha Kitt

23 June
Palace Theatre, Manchester
In the presence of Her Majesty Queen Elizabeth The Queen Mother
Presented by Jack Hylton
Musical Director – Cyril Ornadell
Stage Director – Charles Henry

THE PROGRAMME

'The Opening of the Show' from *The Big Show of 1959* with Paddy Glynn, The Eight Mitchell Singers, The Twenty John Tiller Girls
Tommy Trinder – The Compère
The Peiro Brothers
'Oh Boy!' with Marty Wilde, Cliff Richard, Harry Robinson, Lord Rockingham's II, Cherry Wainer
Benny Hill
Al Read and Jimmy Clitheroe
'Dancing Time' with The Twenty John Tiller Girls, Jean Louis Bert and Ilonka, The Dior Dancers, Belinda Wright with Jelke Yuresha
Jimmy Jewel and Ben Warriss
Roy Castle
BBC Northern Dance Orchestra with Sheila Buxton, Russ Conway, Ronnie Hilton, Jill Day, Marion Ryan
Dickie Henderson
'Palace of Varieties' with Dora Bryan, Aileen Cochrane, Anne Shelton, Terry Wilson
The Children's Ballet, Tower Ballroom Blackpool – 'Be a Clown'
'The Army Game' with Michael Medwin, Alfie Bass, Bill Fraser, Ted Lune, Norman Rossington
Liberace – 'Mr Showmanship'
Arthur Askey
The Hallé Orchestra conducted by Sir John Barbirolli

1959

This year the Royal Variety Performance was for the first time held in Manchester, and one of the features of the show was the presence of the famous Hallé Orchestra conducted by the equally famous Sir John Barbirolli.

The compère for the evening, which was watched with great enthusiasm by the Queen Mother, was one of the very great Royal Variety performers, Tommy Trinder.

There was rich comedy from the likes of Jimmy Jewel and Ben Warriss, Dickie Henderson – and Arthur Askey. Askey got an immediate laugh when he came on with a hurricane lamp on top of a miniature piano. 'You've got to have a gimmick – and I can't afford a candelabra!' he quipped. Perhaps a good-natured swipe at a fellow performer on the night, the extravagant Liberace? Anyway the American pianist – who had missed his Royal Variety début in 1956 because of the Suez Crisis – was happy enough, and he met the Queen Mother after his performance.

Tommy Trinder

1959

The Hallé Orchestra, under the baton of Sir John Barbirolli, was appropriately included in the programme for this Manchester show. In his younger days Sir John had played in the pit of the Wood Green Empire and other theatres, where he had become a great music hall fan. Declining the private dressing room that had been put at his disposal at the Palace, he knocked on the door of the room allotted to Dickie Henderson, Arthur Askey, Roy Castle, Jimmy Jewel and Ben Warriss and asked if he could join them.

Somewhat bemused, they asked Sir John why when he had the comfort of a room all of his own.

'I have always admired and had an affection for stand-up comedians,' he answered, 'and I'd like to share this special night with you. All I ask is a nail on the wall to hang my coat.'

Cliff Richard

Jimmy Clitheroe

Russ Conway

16 May
Victoria Palace, London
In the presence of Her Majesty Queen Elizabeth II and The Duke of Edinburgh
Presented by Jack Hylton
Musical Directors – Billy Ternant and Jack Ansell
Stage Director – Charles Henry

THE PROGRAMME

'Show Place' with **The Ken-Tones, The Jewel Singers, The Showgirls, Sonia Rees, The Croft Twins, The John Tiller Girls, The Crazy Gang**
Bruce Forsyth – The Compère
'Stolen from The Crazy Gang' with **Al Burnett, Diana Dors, Richard Dawson, Jimmy Edwards, Benny Hill, Frankie Howerd, Hattie Jacques, Alfred Marks, Bob Monkhouse, Norman Wisdom**
The Victoria Palace John Tiller Girls Harry Worth
'Focus on Youth' with **Lonnie Donegan and the Lonnie Donegan Group, Adam Faith with the John Barry Seven, Cliff Richard and The Shadows, The Vernons Girls**
'The Fol-De-Rols' with 'The Statues of Liberties', **'The Quorn Quintette'**
Nat 'King' Cole
'Wakey Wakey Tavern' with **Billy Cotton and His Band, Max Bygraves, Russ Conway, Leslie Roberts' 'Silhouettes'**
Robert Horton
'Follow The Bride' with **The Crazy Gang and 'Monsewer' Eddie Gray**
'Jungle Fantasy' with **Kazbek and Zari**
Bruce Forsyth 'Land of Song' with **Ivor Emmanuel and The Pontcanna Children's Choir**
'Tell Me Pretty Maiden' with **Sheila Buxton, Pearl Carr, Alma Cogan, Vera Lynn, Millicent Martin, Joan Regan, Marion Ryan, Janette Scott, Anne Shelton, Yana, Ronnie Carroll, Ronnie Hilton, Bryan Johnson, Benny Lee, Dennis Lotis, Glen Mason, Gary Miller, Jackie Rae, Paul Carpenter**
Charlie Drake with Sheila Eaton, Hughie Green, Sheila Holt, Tom Gillis
Sammy Davis Junior Liberace – 'Mr Showmanship'
'Strolling' and 'We'll Meet Again' with **Bud Flanagan, Vera Lynn and the Entire Company**

1960

The 1960 show at the Victoria Palace will probably always be remembered as Sammy Davis Junior's show.

'In eight electrifying minutes,' wrote the *Daily Sketch*, 'this entertainer made the word "star" seem inadequate.' Certainly the Queen had a breathtaking evening's entertainment. There was wonderful comedy from the Crazy Gang, who greeted Her Majesty in the foyer dressed as Yeomen of the Guards, Harry Worth, Charlie Drake, Jimmy Edwards, Frankie Howerd and Bob Monkhouse. And there was stunning music from Ivor Emmanuel and the Pontcanna Children's Choir with songs from Wales. While, for the young at heart, the organizers had arranged a 'focus on youth' with Lonnie Donegan, Adam Faith and Cliff Richard (who had appeared in Manchester the previous year) and The Shadows.

With that galaxy of talent on display, it was a fitting first year for the Royal Variety Performance to be broadcast on television.

But it was Sammy Davis's night. 'To say he stopped the show,' said *The Stage*, 'is an understatement.'

In fact, it was such an understatement that for once protocol went unheeded and he had eight curtain calls. Those 'in the know' were no doubt aware that curtain calls are not usually part of a Royal Variety Performance.

Lonnie Donegan

1960

The Royal Variety Shows must always go on – even if there is a bomb scare! Two hours before the performance there were reports of an unexploded bomb in the locality. This immediately brought fears of a last-minute cancellation. But, with just a short time to go before curtain up, a bomb disposal unit declared the area safe . . . and the hugely successful show went on.

Having come straight from a rehearsal in Cambridge, Jimmy Edwards was slightly disorientated and unaware that he was due for a full dress rehearsal. He telephoned home, giving instructions concerning the items he needed. 'I want the hunting gear, dear, straight away,' he told his wife. 'We don't need the breeches – that's the joke apparently.'

The finale to this year's show promised to be one of the most spectacular of all time. The entire company, some two hundred in number, were to join the Crazy Gang in 'Strolling', and, dressed in tails and top hats, they emerged from all sides on to the stage. The effect was spell-binding, but not without its backstage hitches.

Liberace and Robert Horton experienced some difficulty getting into their tails and only made it to the wings appropriately attired thanks to the timely intervention of Peter Prichard who happened to be passing their dressing room when he heard cries for assistance. This, incidentally, was the only occasion when Liberace appeared on stage in anything other than his usual dazzling wardrobe.

Sammy Davis Junior was less fortunate with his tails. Although ably assisted by his manager, he could do nothing about the dimensions of the suit, which was several sizes too big. His top hat presented the greatest challenge and the star of the night found himself on stage with the head-band padded with tissues in a lame attempt to keep the hat in place. All was well until it came to the National Anthem, when hats were removed. Out flew the tissues and sailed into the stalls!

If that wasn't bad enough, when the hats were put back on at the end Sammy Davis, to his chagrin, felt his slip down right over his face as the audience, who had restrained themselves commendably until then, slowly dissolved into helpless and uncontrollable laughter.

Ivor Emmanuel

6 November
Prince of Wales, London
In the presence of Her Majesty Queen Elizabeth The Queen Mother
Presented by Bernard Delfont
Musical Director – Harold Collins
Stage Director – Robert Nesbitt

THE PROGRAMME

Bruce Forsyth – The Compère
The *Do-Re-Mi* Boys & Girls in 'Juke Box Rhythm'
Ugo Garrido Jack Benny
Nina & Frederik with The Malcolm Mitchell Trio
Morecambe and Wise
Ballet Trianas Andy Stewart
'And All That Jazz' with Acker Bilk and his Paramount Jazz Band, The Temperance Seven,
Kenny Ball and his Jazzmen
Arthur Haynes
Shirley Bassey
Max Bygraves and the cast in an extract from *Do-Re-Mi*
The Baranton Sisters
Frankie Vaughan
La Compagnie Des Marottes – Ventriloquist
The McGuire Sisters
George Burns
Sammy Davis Junior with Lionel Blair in 'A Gentleman's Hat Shop'
The Crazy Gang with Eddie Gray
Maurice Chevalier

1961

This year's Royal Variety Performance, held at the Prince of Wales Theatre, had a new format, with the number of performers cut by about a third from the previous year, allowing each act to show off the artistes' true individuality.

The Queen Mother's pleasure at the result – Her Majesty has always been a keen variety fan – was evident, not least at a tribute paid to her by Maurice Chevalier.

At his brilliant best as compère this year was Bruce Forsyth. Better known to modern viewers as a TV star, he had a brilliant way with the audience. This year he even managed to upstage Sammy Davis Junior with his own impression of the great American star!

Davis appeared in a dancing scene with Lionel Blair, and there was other American talent on offer too, those comic geniuses Jack Benny and George Burns. The night also saw the wonderful Shirley Bassey in her Royal Variety début.

Shirley Bassey

1961

As an example of some of the problems faced by the director of Royal Variety Performances, Robert Nesbitt recalls having to rehearse the orchestra at eight-thirty on the morning of the show because the plane bringing Sammy Davis Junior into London had been delayed and hadn't arrived until the small hours of the morning. As he explained, in something of an understatement, 'It's a very unfortunate hour to have to rehearse.'

Unhappily, Charlie Drake was unable to appear because of an injury caused during his TV show. Charlie was knocked out during a stunt that went wrong and consequently suffered from loss of memory and severe concussion. He said, 'I don't remember anything of the accident – or much else since.'

There is a generally accepted rule among artistes appearing in the Royal Variety Show that the Royal Box is not addressed directly, but in 1961 there were two notable exceptions to this.

Predictably perhaps, the Crazy Gang lay behind one of these. As many in the audience that night recall, they came on and announced that there was a car blocking a side street outside the theatre. 'I've got the number here,' said Bud Flanagan, 'HRH 1.' Then looking up at the Queen Mother, he said, 'Throw us the keys down, Mam, and we'll move it for you.'

Unknown to Her Majesty, there was someone stationed behind the box to throw a bunch of keys on to the stage, which brought the house down.

The other instance came about when Maurice Chevalier asked Robert Nesbitt whether it would be all right to go over to the Royal Box during the second chorus of 'You Must Have Been a Beautiful Baby' to sing it directly to the Queen Mother.

The answer was, 'From you – yes, it would be all right.' So Chevalier did just that and when it came to the last line he made a charming

Morecambe and Wise

Bruce Forsyth ▲

alteration to end the song 'You must have been a beautiful baby . . . because Majesty look at you now' – a gesture that enchanted all present.

Jack Benny and George Burns joined forces, with Benny in drag, to re-create the popular partnership of George Burns and Gracie Allen. Burns played himself and Benny, in a costume typical of those worn by the late comedienne, gave an hilarious impersonation of Gracie, the two of them recalling for millions of fans the television programme that had made the duo such firm favourites with British audiences. Burn's familiar closing line that invariably followed one of Gracie's ludicrous monologues had become a popular catch-phrase by now and the audience waited with delicious anticipation for him to take a long look, draw on his cigar and say quietly, 'Just say goodnight, Gracie.'

Many members of the audience missed their last tubes and buses due to the show over-running by nearly three-quarters of an hour. To add to their delay, people were prevented from leaving because the foyer was used to present the entertainers to the Royal Party. One theatre-goer was not amused, and complained, 'We could have caught our last tube home if we had got out of the theatre when the curtain fell.'

Frankie Vaughan

Ugo Garrido

29 October
London Palladium
In the presence of Her Majesty Queen Elizabeth II and The Duke of Edinburgh
Presented by Bernard Delfont
Musical Director – Eric Tann
Producer – Robert Nesbitt

THE PROGRAMME

The Palladium Boys and Girls with Janet Mahoney
Harry Secombe
Norman Vaughan – The Compère
The Great Magyar Pusztai Troupe
Dickie Henderson – 'The Man at the Other End'
Johnny Dankworth and his Orchestra with Cleo Laine
Mike & Bernie Winters
The Shadows
Cliff Richard
Eartha Kitt
The Black and White Minstrel Show
'Broadway goes Latin' – Edmundo Ros with Los Hispanos, Margie Ravel, Hector de San Juan, The Arnaldo Dancers
Rudy Cardenas
Frank Ifield
Terry Kendall with Harry Secombe and Norman Vaughan in 'Marching Orders'
Rosemary Clooney Andy Stewart
Sophie Tucker
Bob Hope with Edie Adams

1962

The Queen and Prince Philip were treated to an evening of non-stop entertainment at the Palladium. There was fine singing from two female vocalists who have delighted audiences for many years now – Eartha Kitt and Cleo Laine; comedy from Norman Vaughan, as compère, from Mike and Bernie Winters, and Dickie Henderson, while a surprise hit was the astounding juggling of Rudy Cardenas.

The end of the show belonged to the Americans. First Sophie Tucker in an emotional appearance: a hard act to follow, but who can upstage Bob Hope? The master of comedy soon had the audience fully with him and, aided by Edie Adams, brought the house down.

Sophie Tucker, 'The Last of the Red Hot Hot Mommas', was given a huge ovation at the 1962 show. She was overwhelmed but knew it was a fitting tribute. 'I worked forty years for this night and I reckon I've earned it. It was in 1922 that I made my first appearance in a Royal Variety Show. Tonight they loved it, they loved it, they loved it. The Queen and the Prince were wonderful to me. We had some good laughs together.'

Eartha Kitt was disconcerted by being told not to look at the Queen during her act. Ms Kitt had hoped to direct her song at the Royal Box when uttering the words 'Would you think it a bore if I showed you the door.'

'I'm disappointed I can't look at the Royal Box as I sing,' she said. 'I like to bring people into my act, but it seems it is just not done here. It's not a naughty song – I don't sing naughty songs.'

Mike & Bernie Winters

4 November
Prince of Wales, London
In the presence of Her Majesty Queen Elizabeth The Queen Mother
Presented by Bernard Delfont
Musical Director – Harold Collins
Producer – Robert Nesbitt

THE PROGRAMME
The Billy Petch Dancers
The Clark Brothers
Max Bygraves
Luis Alberto Del Parana and Los Paraguayos
Charlie Drake with Tessa Davees and The Eight Charlies
Susan Maughan
The Beatles
Dickie Henderson
Francis Brunn
Buddy Greco
Nadia Nerina and members of the cast from *Sleeping Beauty*
Joe Loss and his Orchestra with Rose Brennan, Ross McManus, Larry Gretton, The Billy Petch Dancers
'Steptoe & Son' – Wilfred Brambell, Harry H. Corbett
'Pinky & Perky and Company' – Jan and Vlasta Dalibor
Eric Sykes and Hattie Jacques
Michael Flanders and Donald Swann
Marlene Dietrich with Burt Bacarach at the piano
Tommy Steele and members of the *Half A Sixpence* company
Harry Secombe and the *Pickwick* company

1963

This was the night when Beatlemania hit the Royal Variety Performance. By the early sixties the 'Fab Four' from Liverpool were already big stars in the pop world and the presenters of the show at the Prince of Wales shrewdly realized it was time for their Royal show début.

Despite technical problems in rehearsals, it was decidedly more than 'all right' on the night, with all the audience, including the Queen Mother, joining in with the beat. One commentator said, 'Never, in all my years of observing Royal Variety audiences, have I known this usually starchy, on-their-best-behaviour bunch, unbend so quickly and so completely.'

But there was much much more than just the Beatles to enjoy. The bill included Marlene Dietrich and Burt Bacarach, Joe Loss and his orchestra, Charlie Drake, Dickie Henderson and Steptoe & Son – alias Wilfred Brambell and Harry H. Corbett.

Many considered the 1963 show the best yet.

The Beatles

1963

The Beatles attracted crowds of ecstatic fans to the outside of the Prince of Wales. Right through the Sunday of rehearsals the noise of the throng could be heard by the artistes on stage. It was even necessary to construct a screened passageway between the theatre and the hotel next door, where the Beatles were staying, in order to get them in and out of the theatre without being seen.

The effect of the crowds obviously affected the other artistes on the bill and Marlene Dietrich made a point of always being in evidence when the photographers were around!

During rehearsal Paul McCartney managed to get his guitar caught in the curtains, but on the night itself the Beatles took the show by storm and John Lennon passed into Royal Variety history when he made his celebrated suggestion that those in the cheap seats should clap their hands; the rest could just rattle their jewellery.

As part of his act Charlie Drake performed a dance with half a dozen girls, in the course of which he turned to the Royal Box and said, 'I was so pleased to see your horse won at Kempton yesterday, Your Majesty', which was rather a surprising thing to say right in the middle of a Royal Variety Performance.

Not to be outshone by the Beatles, or anyone else, Marlene Dietrich dazzled the audience with a sequin-covered evening dress and enchanted them with a range of songs that included 'Honeysuckle Rose', 'Where Have All The Flowers Gone?' and her all-time favourite 'Lilli Marlene'.

Max Bygraves spoke for many on the bill that night, celebrities in their own right but still capable of being star-struck, when he said, 'I used to see Marlene on the old silver screen and idolize her.'

Michael Flanders and Donald Swann

Marlene Dietrich

2 November
London Palladium
In the presence of Her Majesty Queen Elizabeth II
Presented by Bernard Delfont
Musical Director – Eric Tann
Producer – Robert Nesbitt

THE PROGRAMME

The John Tiller Girls
Tommy Cooper
The Bachelors
Gil Dova – Juggling Act
David Jacobs introduces Cilla Black, Millicent Martin, Kathy Kirby, Brenda Lee
Dennis Spicer – Ventriloquist
Morecambe and Wise
Gracie Fields
The Moiseyev Dance Company – 'Gopak' (Ukranian National Dance)
Ralph Reader and The Gang Show
Jimmy Tarbuck
The Shadows
Cliff Richard
'The Flight of The Urchins' by The Moiseyev Dance Company
Bob Newhart
Lena Horne with The Chico Hamilton Quartette

1964

There were no Beatles this year for the Royal Variety Performance at the Palladium – but there was another rising young star from Liverpool, Jimmy Tarbuck, whose wit and humour captivated the audience, many if not all of whom were seeing him for the first time. 'The greatest, most wonderful day of my life,' he said.

Another much-loved star, Cilla Black, was also making her Royal Variety début and admitted she was very nervous at the prospect. 'I keep dreaming that just before I bow to the Royal Box I fall flat on my face before all those famous people!' She needn't have worried – she and the rest of the show before the Queen were a big success.

Humour came from Morecambe and Wise and the irrepressible Tommy Cooper, with song from Gracie Fields, dance from the Moiseyev Dance Company and juggling from Gil Dova. The Americans were represented by comic Bob Newhart – well-known here for his radio recordings – and singer Lena Horne.

A moving moment came when the Bachelors addressed a line of one of their songs 'I Wouldn't Trade You For The World' to the Queen to spontaneous applause from the audience.

Cilla Black

Jimmy Tarbuck

1964

Bob Newhart became another artiste to experience the anxiety of international travel delays on his way to the Royal Variety Show. His plane had to be diverted to West Germany for some reason and he arrived at the Palladium in the middle of the run-through. Luckily his act involved no music, so he was freed of that anxiety, but it can't have given him the ideal lead into the evening's performance.

There were rum goings-on with the Tiller Girls' black velvet and sequin leotards, which went missing, eventually to be found in the gents' cloakroom! An embarrassed worker at the Palladium dismissed the event a smidgin too defensively. 'We don't really think there was anything sinister about the incident. It was probably some sort of misunderstanding.'

Head Tiller Girl Fay Robinson was not convinced. 'Thank goodness it didn't happen on the night; it was unnerving enough as it was.'

It was a great loss to the variety theatre when Dennis Spicer, a gifted ventriloquist, was killed in a motor accident just days after his success at this year's performance.

One of Robert Nesbitt's innovations as producer of this year's show was to introduce the four popular female recording stars on the bill, Cilla Black, Millicent Martin, Kathy Kirby and Brenda Lee, in a novel way. Each was brought round on a turn of the revolving stage seated in a gleaming sports car – capturing the whole spirit of the Swinging Sixties in one deceptively simple but perfectly judged piece of stagecraft.

The Shadows

Tommy Cooper

8 November
London Palladium
In the presence of Her Majesty Queen Elizabeth II and The Duke of Edinburgh
Presented by Bernard Delfont
Musical Director – Eric Tann
Producer – Robert Nesbitt

THE PROGRAMME

'Meet Me in the Park' with The Kaye Singers, The Palladium Boys and Girls, The Shepherd Singers
Max Bygraves
'Discotheque' with The Dave Clark Five, Dusty Springfield, Johnny Hallyday, Sylvie Vartan, Frank Ifield
Arthur Haynes
'Salute to the Circus' with The Carmenas, Lilly Yokoi
Neville King
Peter Cook and Dudley Moore
Shirley Bassey with Alyn Ainsworth and his Orchestra
'On the Up and Up' with The Palladium Boys and Girls
Hope and Keen
The Kaye Sisters
Spike Milligan
Peter, Paul and Mary
Ken Dodd
Peter Sellers
Tony Bennett
Jack Benny

1965

Zany humour was one of the hallmarks of the 1965 Royal Variety Performance at the Palladium, which was hardly surprising given the names on the bill – Peter Cook, Dudley Moore, Spike Milligan and Peter Sellers, all in the same show!

Prince Charles is of course well-known as a big fan of the Goons and it was interesting that Spike Milligan chose to build a sketch around the young prince's new school at Geelong.

Comedy in more traditional but no less funny style came from Ked Dodd in his Royal Variety début; undoubtedly one of the stars of the show, he capped it all by showing off his fine singing voice.

Shirley Bassey and Tony Bennett – two of the very best in their field – provided classy singing performances, while the 'pop' end of the market was represented by Dusty Springfield and The Dave Clark Five.

A delightful moment came when Bud Flanagan – one of the all-time great Royal Variety performers – made an unscheduled appearance with The Kaye Sisters who sang his song 'Strolling'. To make the occasion even happier it was Bud's forty-first wedding anniversary and his wife Curly was in the audience.

Peter Cook

Dudley Moore

1965

Audrey Bayley was chosen to be the assistant of comedian Peter Sellers. She was delighted, although unclear as to what her role would be, remarking 'It came right out of the blue . . . I had no idea of what I had to do on stage.' Her first task was to wear a brunette wig. The confusion was explained by Peter Sellers. 'There had been rumours that my wife [Britt Ekland] would be in the sketch with me. . . . It wasn't true. And I asked for my partner to be a brunette – to avoid any confusion. Now I've got a blonde just the same. So she'll be wearing a dark wig.'

Ken Dodd the King of the Diddy People had much to celebrate on this night. It was his first royal show and also his thirty-sixth birthday.

The trials and tribulations of deciding what to wear on the night affected several stars. Sylvie Vartan's proposed costume was a white gabardine trouser suit, but would she get the same frosty reception accorded to Vesta Tilley? If she relented to peer pressure, a frock might come in handy. Shirley Bassey would be suitably attired in an evening gown; Dusty Springfield in a floor-length dress of blue beads.

Ken Dodd

Dusty Springfield

14 November
London Palladium
In the presence of Her Majesty Queen Elizabeth The Queen Mother
Presented by Bernard Delfont
Musical Director – Eric Tann
Producer – Robert Nesbitt

THE PROGRAMME

'Down at the Old Bull and Bush' with **The Palladium Boys and Girls and The Bel-Canto Singers**
Des O'Connor – The Compère
The Bachelors
Des O'Connor and Jack Douglas
'A Whole Scene Going' with **Gene Pitney, The Palladium Boys and Girls and the Mike Rabin Group**
Peiro Brothers Gilbert Bécaud Marvo and Dolores Juliette Greco Hugh Forgie
Wayne Newton with Jerry Newton
Kenneth McKellar
Tommy Steele
Nadia Nerina and Christopher Gable with members of the company from *La Fille Mal Gardée*
Henry Mancini
Bal Caron Trio
The Seekers
Frankie Howerd
Matt Monro
Jerry Lewis
Sammy Davis Junior

1966

There were tears, pride and laughter in this year's Royal Variety Performance at the Palladium. Tears, as he sat in the stalls, from French singer Gilbert Bécaud, who had 'lost his voice' and couldn't perform. Pride as the England football team took the stage after their World Cup triumph. And the laughter was almost inevitable with those two masters of comedy Morecambe and Wise, masquerading as Marvo and Dolores. The Queen Mother can hardly ever have seen a more hilarious act than these two with their cod magic act.

And to match the English pride on display there was a rousing scene when Kenneth McKellar was joined by the pipes and drums of the 2nd Battalion Scots Guards after they marched down the aisles to the stage in a rendition of 'Scotland The Brave'.

There were some murmurings of 'not enough ladies' in the show, though this seemed to ignore the presence of the Palladium Girls and the lovely ballerina Nadia Nerina.

Kenneth McKellar

1966

A quote from the 'President's Message' at the beginning of the programme for the 1966 Royal Variety Performance gives an indication of the generosity of so many stars, who over the years have willingly given their time and talents to help the less fortunate members of their profession:

> Sammy Davis Junior has sacrificed a full week's engagements in America, Jerry Lewis is flying here from California. The contingent from New York includes Matt Monro, who is temporarily leaving the Persian Room there, Gilbert Bécaud, whose night's absence causes the closing of the Anta Theatre, and Wayne Newton, who has been released by the Hotel Americana's Royal Box. All our own British stars have made some personal sacrifice too, not merely to help a richly deserving charity, but to honour the debt we all owe to our great variety tradition.

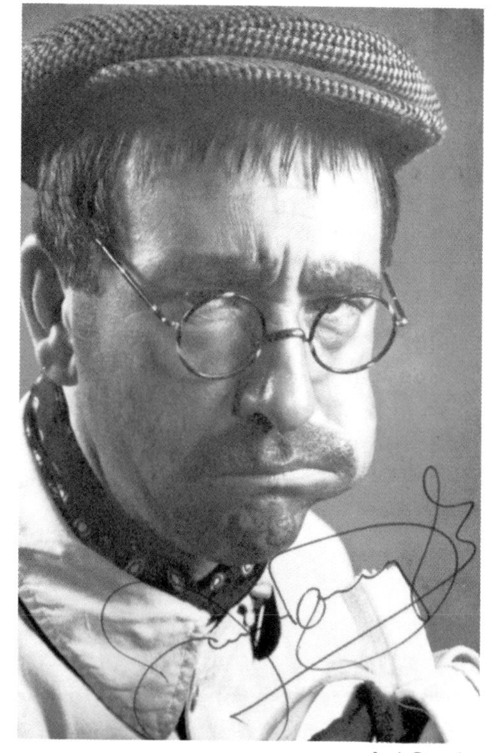

Jack Douglas

The surprise inclusion of the night was the England World Cup team and manager, Alf Ramsey. After holding the World Cup aloft on stage to loud and patriotic applause, the victorious team enjoyed the rest of the show from the stalls.

As compère of the show Des O'Connor was able to work very entertainingly with Jack Douglas, his 'stooge' from many stage and television appearances. Jack appeared as his character Mr Ippititimus, clad in overalls, large boots, cap and steel-rimmed glasses, making his entrance through the audience and interrupting Des O'Connor as he was talking on stage.

'Did I hear some corgies barking?' were his first words.

To which the compère answered, 'What are you doing with that roll of red carpet?' indicating the one Jack Douglas was carrying under his arm.

'I found it in the foyer,' came the reply.

1966

'It's a disgrace, people have been wiping their feet on it.'

They continued in this vein, and when Jack Douglas left the stage he was acclaimed one of the major comic hits of the night.

Prior to the opening of the show, Jack had been asked whether he could change into evening dress for the finale, to be presented to the Royal party after the final curtain. But Des O'Connor pointed out that out of his distinctive Ippititimus 'uniform' he would be unrecognizable, and asked for an exception to be made and Jack Douglas allowed to stay in his familiar costume. Permission was granted.

'Thank you for some marvellous laughter tonight,' the Queen Mother said to Douglas after the show, and then remarking on his distinctive sartorial line added, 'but may I say you're not the smartest man here this evening!'

Frankie Howerd's royal début in 1950 may not have reached his own high standards, but there were no doubts about his success this year. In fact, he went down so well that Lord Snowdon, who was accompanying the Queen Mother, laughed to the extent that he almost fell off his chair. In the presentation line afterwards, Frankie Howerd became one of the few entertainers ever to receive a royal apology, when Lord Snowdon excused himself for laughing so uncontrollably at Frankie's act.

◄ *Des O'Connor*

Frankie Howerd

13 November
London Palladium
In the presence of Her Majesty Queen Elizabeth II and The Duke of Edinburgh
Presented by Bernard Delfont
Musical Director – Eric Tann
Producer – Robert Nesbitt

THE PROGRAMME

The Bluebell Girls – 'Accent on Glamour'
Dickie Henderson
Tanya, The Adorable Elephant
Rolf Harris with the Boys and Girls
Lulu
Sandie Shaw
Val Doonican
Tommy Cooper
Harry Secombe
Rumanian National Dance Company and Orchestra
'Feather Fantasy' – The Bluebell Girls
The Rockin' Berries
Ken Dodd
Vikki Carr
Mireille Mathieu
Tom Jones
Bob Hope

1967

'Bring on the Dancing Girls' could have been the theme of the 1967 Royal Variety Performance, held once again at the Palladium. After an apparent 'shortage' of ladies in the previous year's show, there was a welcome number this year. It began with the curtain rising to reveal the Bluebell Girls etched in silhouette before they went into their routine.

This took place before the Queen – Prince Philip, returning from an engagement in Canada, was just too late to see them. 'Have I missed the Bluebells?' he asked as he took his seat in the box. Yes he had, but there were more dancing girls to come accompanying Australian entertainer Rolf Harris, and later the Rumanian Dance Company and Orchestra.

Two notable debutantes were pop singers Sandie Shaw and Lulu, while the comedy high spots were provided by Ken Dodd (and his Diddy People) and Tommy Cooper. The evening was brought to an amusing climax by Bob Hope.

Lulu

1967

Sandie Shaw was wearing a special outfit to meet the Queen – a velvet knickerbocker suit trimmed with white lace – but during Sandie's performance, she was wearing her more usual apparel: a magenta mini-dress and, of course, her trademark of appearing barefoot. On being asked how she came to decide on the all-important outfit, Sandie answered, 'A mini is fine on stage but I am told it would be more elegant to be presented to the Queen in something a little more special.'

Joanna Cran, one of the Rolf Harris dancers, nearly had a very unfortunate accident. She fell through a trapdoor during a rehearsal, but luckily managed to hold on to the sides until she was pulled up. Asked about her experience, the dancer showed true spirit. 'I was terrified, but I was even more frightened I might not be able to appear in the show.'

Without doubt one of the great hits of the evening was Tanya the baby elephant (all 1,600 pounds of her). Tanya appeared with Dickie Henderson and was soon a great favourite backstage. She became a regular frequenter of the stage-door, waiting there patiently while her keeper slipped out for a drink.

Tanya and the stage-door man became great chums and before popping out himself, he would hang up his jacket in which a couple of sweets were always carefully secreted in a pocket. 'Now don't go near my jacket,' he would warn Tanya before he left. But she soon learned that there was something tasty to be found if she searched through the pockets and the sweets never went undiscovered.

In the end a little notice appeared asking the company to curtail their generosity lest Tanya put on weight. On the night of the show Tanya was given a tremendous round of applause when she held up a card reading 'I work for peanuts'.

Rolf Harris

Val Doonican

18 November
London Palladium
In the presence of Her Majesty Queen Elizabeth The Queen Mother
Presented by Bernard Delfont
Musical Director – Robert Lowe
Producer – Robert Nesbitt

THE PROGRAMME

Aimi Macdonald and Lionel Blair, with the *Lady Be Good* dancers and Joe Chisolm
Des O'Connor
Arthur Askey
Valente Valente
Morecambe and Wise
Sacha Distel
Czechoslovakian State Song and Dance Ensemble
Ted Rogers
Manitas De Plata and Company
Engelbert Humperdinck
Agnes O'Connell's London Irish Girl Pipers
Val Doonican
Petula Clark
Ron Moody
André Tahon and Company
Diana Ross and The Supremes

1968

This Royal Variety Performance, staged at the Palladium, was considered by many to be the best for some time. Indeed, that was the view of the Queen Mother, by now a seasoned connoisseur of music hall and variety.

Her Majesty was joined in the Royal Box by the youthful Prince Charles, Princess Anne, Princess Margaret and the Earl of Snowdon. They were treated to some fine humour, notably from Frankie Howerd and Mike Yarwood, both late stand-ins for Morecambe and Wise who had to withdraw after Eric Morecambe was taken ill. Musical entertainment came from the superb flamenco guitarist Manitas De Plata, the young heart-throb Sacha Distel, Petula Clark and Diana Ross and the Supremes, as well as Engelbert Humperdinck.

A comic who marked himself as a star of the future was the young Ted Rogers, now well-known to TV viewers as a popular game show host.

Diana Ross and The Supremes

Aimi Macdonald and Lionel Blair

1968

Diana Ross used this opportunity to make a moving tribute to black civil rights leader, Martin Luther King – who had been assassinated earlier in the year – during her performance with The Supremes. She was able to introduce this in the middle of singing *Somewhere*, speaking in time to the music, 'Let our efforts be as determined as those of Dr Martin Luther King, who had a dream that all God's children . . . could join hands and sing . . . There's a place for us, black and white, Jew and gentile . . . and the world of Martin Luther King and his ideals.'

The business of performing weighed heavily on Petula Clark's shoulders. This was due to her costume – a white evening dress that hit the scales at forty pounds! It was small wonder that some acerbic wit gave it the nickname 'suit of armour'.

There was misery for the front-line dancer from the Czechoslovakian Ensemble, Eva Cumroaba, who was heartbroken at not being able to perform as she had a back injury. It may have been tempting to go on with the show but when ordered by doctors to rest, there was nothing she could do but lie back and enjoy the night's entertainment on the television.

Engelbert Humperdinck

Petula Clark

10 November
London Palladium
In the presence of Her Majesty Queen Elizabeth II and The Duke of Edinburgh
Presented by Bernard Delfont
Musical Director – Russell Wright
Producer – Robert Nesbitt

THE PROGRAMME

Des O'Connor with The Palladium Girls
The Veterans
Roy Castle
Cilla Black
Danny La Rue
Shari Lewis
Harry Secombe
Ginger Rogers, Barry Kent, Sheila Keith and members of the chorus in an excerpt from *Mame*
Buddy Rich and his Orchestra
Moira Anderson
Scène de Ballet
Ronnie Corbett
Mireille Mathieu
Herb Alpert and his Tijuana Brass
Frankie Howerd
Tom Jones with Johnnie Spence and his Orchestra and the Mike Sammes' Singers

1969

If the 1969 Royal Variety Performance could be described as a 'drag' it was only because Danny La Rue stole the show at the Palladium! His act was one of the big successes of the night, but the Queen and Prince Philip had much else to enjoy besides. Making his début was Ronnie Corbett, now a popular old favourite in 'royal shows', and there was a glittering performance from ventriloquist Shari Lewis with 'Lamp Chop', her dummy.

The audience also thrilled to Ginger Rogers and other members of the cast from *Mame*, and later to the breathtaking voice of French singer Mireille Mathieu.

Des O'Connor, who appeared first with the Palladium Girls, 'warned' the audience that it was going to be a fast show with no compère – and so it proved to be, with act after talented act flashing before their eyes. To cap it off was the powerful singing of Tom Jones.

Derek Batey, Ronnie Corbett and Lew Lane

1969

Ronnie Corbett was sporting a black eye when he appeared before the Queen, and it was not a joke! The accident happened during a car crash as he was driven home after a night out. He recalled the incident with the precision of a rally driver: 'I was thrown against the fascia of the car. The rim of my glasses hit me under the right eye.' However, Ronnie had the good luck to be nursed by Danny La Rue, who bathed the eye in champagne.

The advent of colour television posed new problems for this show, that were to be solved by somewhat unusual methods. Thelma Taylor was the vital component who helped ITV get the colour balance exactly right. Ms Taylor, a dancer and singer by profession (although not needing those skills for this particular part), wore a green dress, pink stole and white boots. If that didn't help the newfangled colour cameras, nothing would!

Danny La Rue

A big hit of the evening was Danny La Rue. His act was well received, especially his impersonations of Margot Fonteyn and Sandie Shaw. Her Majesty the Queen told him after the show, 'My gosh, your costume changes were fantastic. I only wish I could dress as quickly as you.'

The hectic schedules of leading international artistes caused headaches for Robert Nesbitt again in 1969 when Herb Alpert and his band were delayed by fog in Vienna and weren't able to arrive at the Palladium until after the run-through had ended. With a gruelling day already completed and the show only a couple of hours away, the producer then had to set about checking technical details like sound and lighting, not to mention making the ever cheerful Mr Alpert and his colleagues feel welcome and truly part of the performance. As Robert Nesbitt well remembers, 'We never saw them in the context of the show until the actual performance!'

Tom Jones

9 November
London Palladium
In the presence of Her Majesty Queen Elizabeth The Queen Mother
Presented by Bernard Delfont
Musical Director – Eric Tann
Producer – Robert Nesbitt

THE PROGRAMME

The Pamela Devis Dancers
Max Bygraves
Peter Noone and Herman's Hermits with the Pamela Devis Dancers
Freddie Starr
Rostal and Schaefer
Sandy Powell with Kay White
Dionne Warwick
The Doriss Girls
Syd Lawrence and his Orchestra
Leslie Crowther
The Black Theatre of Prague
Caterina Valente
Marty Feldman, Tim Brooke-Taylor
Andy Williams

1970

There was a true variety of talent on offer when the Queen Mother settled down to watch the 1970 Royal Variety Performance at the Palladium. Her Majesty saw the new, vital talent of impressionist Freddie Starr, and the puppeteering of the Black Theatre of Prague; heard the smooth sound of Syd Lawrence and his orchestra, and, rounding off a successful show, the urbane, sophisticated American singer Andy Williams.

All this contrasting talent was held together beautifully by the relaxed style of Max Bygraves, always a big hit with the occupants of the Royal Box.

Wonderful playing of classical music came from the pianists Rostal and Schaefer, pop from Peter Noone and Herman's Hermits, while for light relief there was humour from Marty Feldman and Tim Brooke-Taylor, the latter perhaps best known as one of the Goodies.

The 'President's Message' that year made the point that, apart from Max Bygraves, 'all the remaining artistes on the stage of the London Palladium are appearing in their first Royal Variety Performance, making it in one sense a 'première'.

'That, I think, has a newness which will give a warm fillip to those who firmly believe that there is great talent abounding amongst us today, waiting in the wings for their chance to scale the heights.'

The Black Theatre of Prague

Syd Lawrence and his Orchestra

1970

One of the virtually unknown performers who was feeling very apprehensive about the show was Freddie Starr. Realizing how nervous he was, Billy Marsh, a Life Governor of the Entertainment Artistes' Benevolent Fund and a key figure in the creation and production of the Royal Variety Performance for many years, took him up to the BBC to see Morecambe and Wise. This did the trick, for when Freddie Starr went on stage quite early in the bill that night, he nearly stopped the show. His impression of stars like Mick Jagger and Norman Wisdom had the audience calling for more and he was rewarded by being called back to take a second bow.

On the basis of that night alone it was just as well that he had chosen not to take the counsel offered by his manager, who admitted himself, 'To think that I once advised him that he should never go solo. He used to do his act in front of a pop group and I told him that I didn't think he ought to go it alone.'

Sandy Powell, whose catch-phrase was 'Can you hear me, Mother?' had last appeared at the Royal Variety Show thirty-five years before. He was the replacement for Mary Hopkin who had to withdraw because of her television commitments. Sandy was delighted to accept, although very surprised. 'I had actually applied for tickets and was astonished when they asked me to appear.'

Sandy Powell

15 November
London Palladium
In the presence of Her Majesty Queen Elizabeth II
Presented by Bernard Delfont
Musical Director – Eric Tann
Producer – Robert Nesbitt

THE PROGRAMME

The Young Generation
The Villams
Bruce Forsyth
Dailey and Wayne
The Stupids
Lovelace Watkins
Norman Collier
Hughie Green
The Little Angels of Korea
Jack Parnell and his Orchestra
The New Seekers
The New Dollys
Ken Goodwin
Sacha Distel and Stephane Grappelli
Tommy Cooper
Shirley Bassey

1971

As always, the value of a compère was shown in the 1971 Royal Variety Performance held at the Palladium, with Bruce Forsyth ably holding together the diverse package of acts on show, while injecting humour of his own.

The evening got off to an energetic start with the Young Generation literally stepping into their dancing boots on stage. The pace was hardly less frantic with an unusual act from Sweden called The Stupids. Their comic acrobatic skills caused one commentator to liken them to 'Keystone Kops on LSD'!

Distinguished music came from singer Sacha Distel and brilliant musician Stephane Grappelli, before Shirley Bassey ended the show in her own inimitable style.

Once again, Tommy Cooper, with his very distinctive humour, took many of the honours for comedy.

The New Seekers

The Little Angels of Korea

1971

Although the Royal Variety Performance is a charity show, the stars do not expect to have to pay for the privilege of appearing in it! Comedian Norman Collier found himself one hundred pounds out of pocket when he was asked to perform in the show. He had been booked by the Black & White Minstrels for that night and in order to take part in the Royal Variety Performance he had to pay fellow comedian Derek Dene to take his place.

Tommy Cooper, a comedian who was always full of surprises, had a special one for the organizers of the 1971 show. After rehearsing his act, Robert Nesbitt checked with him that what they had just seen was exactly what he was going to be doing on the night. 'It's going to run five minutes?' questioned the director. 'You haven't left anything out, have you? That's what we'll be getting?'

Tommy Cooper said that was what he was going to be doing.

Imagine Robert Nesbitt's astonishment, then, when, come the evening performance, Tommy went on and did just three minutes – something almost unheard-of among comedians at a Royal Variety Performance!

The Little Angels of Korea were fifty children who appeared on stage in rather charming costumes and sang as engagingly as their name implied. However, they did have trouble with the words of the National Anthem. Tears were nearly shed as they tried in vain to pronounce the letter 'Q'. No matter how often Robert Nesbitt gently corrected them, 'queen' kept coming out as 'king'. When it was obvious that Anglo-Korean relations wouldn't be furthered by labouring the point, the issue was left to one side and the Little Angels saluted Her Majesty that night in their own inimitable style.

Hughie Green

Lovelace Watkins

30 October
London Palladium
In the presence of Her Majesty Queen Elizabeth The Queen Mother
Presented by Bernard Delfont
Musical Director – Russell Wright
Producer – Robert Nesbitt

THE PROGRAMME

Los Diablos Del Bombo
Dickie Henderson
Mike Yarwood
Elton John
'Salute the Stars' with Danny La Rue, David Ellen, The Tommy Shaw Dancers, The Derek New Singers
Liberace
Trio Hoganas
Rod Hull and Emu
The Jackson Five
Jack Jones
Ken Dodd
From *Till Death Us Do Part* with Warren Mitchell, Dandy Nichols, Anthony Booth, Una Stubbs
Carol Channing

1972

A new-look Royal Variety Performance proved a big hit at the Palladium. The programme was more 'personal' than previous ones, with fewer big set-pieces in favour of a more one-to-one approach.

And for the Queen Mother there was much individual talent to enjoy. Dickie Henderson, a polished compère, suffered at the hands (or rather beak) of Rod Hull and Emu; Ken Dodd and Mike Yarwood, two big TV stars by this time, delighted the audience, while there was plenty of glamour from Danny La Rue, Liberace and singer Jack Jones. Nor was there a shortage of pop with the famous Jackson Five – one of which of course was Michael Jackson – and the versatile Elton John. With eight acts making their début it was a very successful night.

Only the sketch from the *Till Death Us Do Part* cast failed to take off fully as hoped, showing that it is sometimes difficult to make the transition from television sit-coms to a live stage act in one move.

Elton John

1972

The BBC celebrated its fiftieth anniversary in 1972, and the recording of the Royal Variety Performance was broadcast on Sunday 5 November on BBC television, highlighting the commencement of a week of Golden Jubilee celebrations the corporation was holding. Indeed, the show was held slightly earlier than usual in order 'to acknowledge and herald the historic event'.

The glittering star Liberace was certainly the sartorial highlight of the evening. Always out to excel in the costume stakes, for this evening's entertainment Liberace wore an electrically illuminated suit, costing £5,000. Fervent fans of the pianist were praying that there would not be a power cut!

Not to be outdone by Liberace, Danny La Rue's costume bill came to £7,000! It seemed that the female impersonator had the upper hand as he could boast of four costume changes during his act.

An appearance in the Royal Variety Show does not necessarily in itself bring wealth and glamour. The hard facts of life have to be faced prosaically. Anthony Booth from the popular television series *Till Death Us Do Part*, signed on the dole the very day he appeared in this year's show, for he needed the unemployment benefit to keep him going during the lean months when he was not able to find work. A life treading the boards is not all it's cracked up to be, as Anthony explained: 'I know it's going from the sublime to the ridiculous when I have to go on the dole after a successful TV series but that's the way it is for an awful lot of actors;' – a lesson that drives home the importance of the work of the EABF (formerly VABF).

Liberace

Jack Jones

26 November
London Palladium
In the presence of Her Majesty Queen Elizabeth II and The Duke of Edinburgh
Presented by Bernard Delfont
Musical Director – Gordon Rose
Producer – Robert Nesbitt

THE PROGRAMME

The Dougie Squires Second Generation
Dick Emery
Francis Van Dyke
Philippe Genty and Company
Cliff Richard
Les Dawson
Rudolf Nureyev and Lynn Seymour
The Dougie Squires Second Generation – 'Side by Side'
Peters and Lee
José Luis Moreno
Nana Mouskouri and The Athenians
Ronnie Corbett
Duke Ellington and his Orchestra

1973

Astonishingly, nine out of the eleven acts at the 1973 Royal Variety Performance at the Palladium (the twenty-fifth to be held there) were making their débuts.

This made no difference to the quality of the evening's entertainment, the Queen and Prince Philip as usual treated to some wonderful performances.

Les Dawson, the droll, dead-pan comic was a major success story on the night and appeared to be very popular with the Duke of Edinburgh in particular.

The contrast could hardly have been greater with the appearance of two great names of ballet, Lynn Seymour and Rudolf Nureyev – truly a night of variety!

One of the 'old hands' of Royal Variety Shows, Ronnie Corbett was at his relaxed best before leading on to one of the high spots of the evening, Duke Ellington and his Orchestra.

Rudolf Nureyev and Lynn Seymour

1973

To 1973 belongs one of the most frequently told stories of the Royal Variety Show, centred on the big name of the night, Duke Ellington.

Due to yet another travel mix-up, this time *en route* from Kenya, he and his musicians arrived after the run-through, with only an hour and a half to go before the curtain was due to go up.

While some of his musicians went to the theatre to take notes from Robert Nesbitt and find out what they were supposed to be doing, Duke Ellington, who was not young by that stage, retired to bed exhausted.

To add to the mounting chaos the band's musical instruments were still sitting in the customs area at Heathrow! The show had been running a nail-biting fifteen minutes before the instruments and band clothes finally arrived.

It wasn't until the interval that Robert Nesbitt actually saw Duke Ellington, lying stretched out in his dressing room in the dark. They went through the details of his entry through the curtain before the band was revealed.

When it came to what they were going to play, the director was happy to leave it to Ellington to decide. His only advice was that the Duke of Edinburgh's favourite tune was 'I'll Take the A Train'. Bearing in mind that he was talking to someone who hadn't even been able to set foot on the stage it was pretty nerve-racking.

Great artiste that he was, Ellington carried it off perfectly; stepping through the curtain to take his bow, he turned round and as the curtains opened to reveal his musicians he went straight into 'I'll Take the A Train', which was a great way to start.

The popular and articulate singer Nana Mouskouri (she can speak more than seven languages) was sadly unable to appear in this year's show. She had a throat infection.

Duke Ellington

Douglas Squires

1973

Dick Emery

18 November
London Palladium
In the presence of Her Majesty Queen Elizabeth The Queen Mother
Presented by Bernard Delfont
Musical Director – Eric Tann
Producer – Robert Nesbitt

THE PROGRAMME

'A Salute to Vaudeville' with Noele Gordon, Esmaralda and Diane Theron, Susanne and Fudi, Nino and Wendy Frediani, Lilian Kenny, Linda Novaro, Skating Valentines, The Schaller Brothers
Ted Rogers
The Hungarian State Dance Company
Billy Dainty
Josephine Baker
Paul Melba
The Dance Theatre of Harlem – Excerpts from 'Forces of Rhythm'
Paper Lace
George Carl
Roy Castle
Perry Como with The Tony Mansell Singers
Jack Parnell and his Orchestra

1974

For the 1974 Royal Variety Performance at the Palladium there were some important differences. First, the Variety Artistes' Benevolent Fund officially changed its name to the Entertainment Artistes' Benevolent Fund, marking its help for a wider spectrum of show business.

Second, the Royal Show had a female compère – or commère to use the correct word – for the first time. This was Noele Gordon, who had starred in previous shows herself, and it was Ms Gordon who introduced the nostalgic celebration 'A Salute To Vaudeville'.

Ted Rogers, who had also appeared before in a Royal Show, successfully followed with his comedy routine. Fast and furious dancing came from the Dance Theatre of Harlem, and the evening was given a smooth, polished end by the outstanding American singer Perry Como.

Noele Gordon

Josephine Baker

1974

This was the night that the comedian Billy Dainty made the Queen Mother cry – with tears of amusement, that is. Dainty's impersonations of Fred Astaire, Gene Kelly and Rudolf Nureyev were more than the Queen Mother could bear. After the show, she was reported as saying 'I think he's marvellous. I was crying with laughter.'

Billy Dainty

10 November
London Palladium
In the presence of Her Majesty Queen Elizabeth II and The Duke of Edinburgh
Presented by Bernard Delfont
Musical Director – Eric Tann
Producer – Robert Nesbitt

THE PROGRAMME

Bruce Forsyth
Kwa Zulu – African Song and Dance Company
Kris Kremo – Juggler
'Choir Practice' from *Dad's Army* with Arthur Lowe, John Le Mesurier, Clive Dunn, Arnold Ridley, Ian Lavender, Bill Pertwee, Frank Williams, Edward Sinclair, John Bardon, Hamish Roughead, Joan Cooper, Pamela Cundell, Janet Davies
Count Basie and his Orchestra
Larry Parker – Comedian
Michael Crawford and the company of *Billy*
Dukes and Lee with The Trackers
Ruth Welting – Soprano
Telly Savalas with Gus Savalas, Inez Anthony, Rebecca Lewis, Alexandria Brown, Christine Gow, Susan Buckner, Carol Lorham
Charles Aznavour
The Rhos Male Voice Choir
Harry Secombe
Vera Lynn

1975

It was *Billy*'s year as the incredibly versatile Michael Crawford, with other members of the Drury Lane show, won over the audience of the 1975 Royal Variety Performance at the Palladium. Crawford's talent and sheer ebullience certainly pleased the Queen and Prince Philip in an evening of wide-ranging talent.

For sheer scale the splendour of the Kwa Zulu African song and dance company and the Rhos Male Voice Choir from Wales, who featured in the finale with Royal Variety veterans Harry Secombe and Vera Lynn, made magnificent entertainment. More music came from Count Basie and his orchestra and light comedy from the team of the television series, *Dad's Army*. One of the big hits of the night was the French singer, Charles Aznavour.

Michael Crawford

1975

There was something of a furore over whether the female dancers in *Kwa Zulu* could appear topless as they did in their West End show.

What would the Queen think? Would she be offended? These questions were answered by a spokesperson from Buckingham Palace, very tactfully putting forward Her Majesty's reassurance that 'The Queen has seen topless ladies before.'

Michael Crawford made a death-defying entrance, travelling across the stage by means of a rope tied around one ankle. No wonder he was insured for £150,000 against accident!

Telly Savalas, the actor best-known for his role as Kojak in the American cop series of the same name was on the wrong side of the law for once. Mr Savalas was frisked by security guards before he was allowed into the building for his dress rehearsal. Perhaps they thought he looked like a suspicious character. Whatever the reason, it demonstrated the very strict security at the Palladium that year, following a number of bomb scares that autumn.

The lot of the producer of a Royal Variety Performance is not always the easiest – particularly when dealing with artistes from many different countries – and in 1975 Robert Nesbitt discovered that even the most innocent of observations can somehow become stretched out of their true focus.

As with many of the artistes on the bill, he gave notes to Charles Aznavour, who had sung three songs in rehearsal as he intended doing on the night. Robert felt that they all had a rather similar slow tempo and suggested that it might work better if the middle song was substituted with something slightly livelier, to introduce a fresh rhythm.

A fairly lengthy debate ensued, the result of which was Charles Aznavour agreeing to

Count Basie

Telly Savalas

replace his second song with something a little quicker. What took Robert Nesbitt totally by surprise was a report in one of the newspapers the following morning alleging that the song had been removed because it had a homosexual content that would not have been appropriate in front of the Queen – which wasn't an aspect of the number that had even entered Robert Nesbitt's mind!

Eve Boswell and Charles Aznavour

15 November
London Palladium
In the presence of Her Majesty Queen Elizabeth The Queen Mother
Presented by Bernard Delfont
Musical Director – Ronnie Hazelhurst
Producer – Robert Nesbitt

THE PROGRAMME

Max Bygraves in 'Back in my Childhood Days' with The Lionel Blair Dancers
Dance Theatre of Harlem in 'Spiritual Suite'
Los Reales Del Paraguay – The Music of Latin America
Roger de Courcey and 'Nookie' – Ventriloquist
Lena Zavaroni – Singer, with The Nigel Lythgoe Dancers
Dance Theatre of Harlem in 'The Beloved'
Gilbert Bécaud and his Musicians
Dance Theatre of Harlem – 'Dougla'
Tom O'Connor – Comedian
Dawson Chance – Puppeteer
Wayne King – Pianist
Mike Yarwood – Impressionist
Shirley Bassey

1976

On paper the 1976 Royal Variety Performance at the Palladium looked to have one of the smallest cast lists for a long time. But what it lacked in quantity it more than made up for in quality in a talented line-up.

In the first-ever live TV broadcast of the show, Los Reales Del Paraguay with Latin-American music and the Dance Theatre of Harlem provided ideal visual spectacles. Humour came from Tom O'Connor and the by now established Royal Variety performer Mike Yarwood.

French singer Gilbert Bécaud, who had missed an earlier show, at last had his chance to show the Queen Mother what he could do. And, rounding off a successful night, was the ever-popular singer from Tiger Bay, Shirley Bassey.

Shirley Bassey

1976

The Queen Mother seemed to be mesmerized by the hypnotic eyes of Nookie Bear. 'The Queen Mother spoke with me for a long time,' said the ventriloquist Roger de Courcey, 'and kept referring to the eyes of Nookie, my bear. She was quite fascinated with them.'

The prospect of broadcasting the Royal Variety Performance live was intriguing. To some there was the tantalizing possibility of seeing how any hitches that would have been edited out of the shows in previous years were really dealt with. Others were simply satisfied with enjoying the night's entertainment at the same time as the theatre audience. One viewer, Mrs Queenie Perkins, quoted in the *Daily Mirror* the following morning, spoke for millions when she said, 'It was certainly worth watching. You look at the show differently when you know it hasn't been pre-recorded. It becomes that much more enjoyable.'

Roger de Courcey

The Dance Theatre of Harlem

21 November
London Palladium
In the presence of Her Majesty Queen Elizabeth II and The Duke of Edinburgh
Presented by Lew Grade and Bernard Delfont
Producers – Garry Smith and Dwight Hemion
Musical Director – Jack Parnell
Stage Director – Robert Nesbitt

THE PROGRAMME

Bob Hope – The Host
Julie Andrews
Paul Anka
Pam Ayres
Harry Belafonte
Brotherhood of Man
Tommy Cooper
Alan King
Cleo Laine with John Dankworth, John Williams
Little and Large
Shirley MacLaine
Jim Henson's Muppets
Rudolph Nureyev

1977

To celebrate Her Majesty the Queen's Silver Jubilee a Royal Gala Performance was arranged at the Palladium. For this special show I joined forces with my brother, Lew Grade, to create a programme with strong transatlantic appeal.

'Many of America's greatest artistes will be appearing in this unique Gala Performance,' we said in our joint message in the programme, 'in tribute and salutation, from the United States of America, to honour the twenty-fifth anniversary of the accession to the Throne by Her Majesty the Queen. Fittingly, along with the American artistes, British stars will be appearing.'

Although the Entertainment Artistes' Benevolent Fund was not the sole beneficiary of this unique show – sharing the estimated £1,000,000 benefit with the Young Men's Christian Association, the Queen's Silver Jubilee Appeal Fund and other charities – it stood to realize a sum substantially in excess of that in any previous year.

It was a big show in every way, with a star-studded line up and a projected running time of four hours – twice the length of any previous show. And Bob Hope was a perfect choice to play host for a night of truly royal entertainment.

Stars abounded, both animate and inanimate. The Muppets were a great hit, along with names like Rudolph Nureyev, Tommy Cooper and Julie Andrews.

Newer talents were also in evidence, among them Little and Large, Pam Ayres and the Brotherhood of Man.

One of the undoubted highlights was Cleo Laine, Johnnie Dankworth and the guitarist John Williams appearing together – a performance that was greeted with rapture by the audience.

Little and Large

1977

As well as my brother having joined forces with me to create the show, the Silver Jubilee Gala was particularly memorable for another important family connection. Reg Swinson, the General Secretary of the Entertainment Artistes' Benevolent Fund and a man whose courtesy and attention to the fine details of etiquette that help to retain the status of the Royal Variety shows year after year is well known throughout show business, graciously suggested that our mother should present the bouquet to Her Majesty on arrival at the foyer.

In answer to her question as to what she should say to the Queen, Reg gently suggested, 'Just say good evening.'

'But supposing the Queen asks me about my boys?' our mother reputedly asked!

Bing Crosby had been billed as joint compère with Bob Hope, but sadly he died just five weeks before the performance. Evidently affected by the loss, Bob Hope nevertheless went ahead with the show and paid tribute to 'a man who meant an awful lot to me and an awful lot to the world. He was the greatest entertainer of them all.'

Kathryn Crosby, Bing's widow, was in the audience and stood up to take the tribute for her husband.

For this special occasion, Kermit the Frog was in a white tie, and bowed as low as amphibians can.

Miss Piggy came up with some memorable lines, such as 'Kissy-kissy to the Queen', and was especially attentive to Prince Charles.

Well-received as Bob Hope undeniably was, his performance did not pass without some mild criticism. One reviewer noted that while his apparent ease and langour came over well on television, the theatre audience's view was often hampered by his cue cards!

Shirley MacLaine

Bob Hope

13 November
London Palladium
In the presence of Her Majesty Queen Elizabeth The Queen Mother
Presented by Bernard Delfont and Louis Benjamin
Musical Director – Gordon Rose
Producer – Robert Nesbitt

THE PROGRAMME

David Jacobs

'Before Your Very Eyes' – **Arthur Askey with The John McCarthy Singers, Lionel Blair, Leslie Crowther, Bobby Crush, Charlie Drake, Cyril Fletcher, Rolf Harris, John Inman, David Nixon, The Beverley Sisters, Marti Caine, Wendy Craig, Sandra Dickenson, Esther Rantzen, Dilys Watling, June Whitfield**

Pepe and his Friends presented by **Roger Stevenson and Harry G. Stuart**

'Not a Lot' – **Paul Daniels**

'Harry's World of Music' with **Harry Secombe, The King's Singers, Mary O'Hara, Showaddywaddy**

'Music Hall Nights' with **Danny La Rue and members of the Players Theatre**

'From Over the Border' with **The Krankies, Andy Stewart, The Regimental Band, Pipes and Drums of the Royal Scots Dragoon Guards, Moira Anderson, The Scottish Ballet**

'Strike Up the Band' with **The National Youth Jazz Orchestra, Acker Bilk, Kenny Ball**

'A Nostalgic Musical Flashback' with **Max Bygraves:** 'The Twenties' – **The Kaye Sisters;** 'The Thirties' – **The Nolan Sisters;** 'The Forties' – **Anne Shelton**

'On with the Dance' with **Wayne Sleep, Lesley Collier, Diane Langton**

'Oggi, Oggi, Oggi' **Max Boyce** with his team

1978

Twenty years after the first Royal Variety Performance that I presented, the 1978 show marked my swan song. Although I had been paid the signal honour by the EABF of being appointed its first Life President, I was now handing over the responsibility of presenting the shows to Louis Benjamin, a Life Governor who had been closely associated with the Royal Variety Performances of previous years and was now donning the mantle of presenter in his own right, although in 1978 we worked together in this capacity.

It was also comforting that the last show I was to present would be a tribute to Her Majesty Queen Elizabeth The Queen Mother. To this end there was an all-British bill with a strong contingent from north of the border, one of the sets depicting the Castle of May.

David Jacobs was compère and introduced a colourful 'Day at Ascot' scene.

A musical theme was struck with 'Harry's World of Music' featuring Harry Secombe, with the King's Singers, Mary O'Hara and the pop group Showaddywaddy.

Later, to the delight of the Queen Mother, came the Music Hall theme, with Danny La Rue and members of the Players Theatre. And there was a nostalgic musical 'flashback' with Max Bygraves, assisted by the Nolan Sisters, the Kaye Sisters and Anne Shelton. Next came dance led by the super-talented Wayne Sleep.

Max Boyce was another hit with his own very Welsh brand of humour.

The programme seemed to achieve its desired effect, for the Queen Mother told one of the show's evergreen stars, Arthur Askey, 'I think this is the best "royal show" I have ever seen.'

Max Boyce

1978

A great favourite for many years, Gracie Fields made a surprise comeback to the Palladium. She was especially flown in from her home in Capri to sing her best-known song, 'Sally'.

The critics of the Royal Variety Performance were keen to point out that it seemed to cater for the over-fifty age group. But what was wrong with that in this special year? 'It was a show for the older generation,' said Gertrude Skelton, a member of the audience.

Another satisfied customer was Peggy Davies, 'I liked it . . . but then I'm sixty-eight.'

Gracie Fields

The Krankies

June Whitfield

26 November
Theatre Royal, Drury Lane
In the presence of Her Majesty Queen Elizabeth II
Presented by Louis Benjamin
Musical Director – Gordon Rose
Producer – Norman Maen

THE PROGRAMME

Elaine Stritch with The Norman Maen Dancers
'Nick! Nick!' – **Jim Davidson**
James Galway – The Man with the Golden Flute
Red Buttons
Ned Sherrin presents 'Song by Song by Drury': 'Showboat 1928' with **Millicent Martin, David Kernan, Julia McKenzie**; 'Oklahoma 1947' with **Marti Caine**; 'The Boys from Syracuse 1963' with **Julia McKenzie and The English National Opera Chorus**; 'Cavalcade 1931' with **Elisabeth Welch**; 'The World of Ivor Novello' with **Hinge and Bracket**; 'My Fair Lady 1958' with **Millicent Martin**; 'Alan Jay Lerner Medley' with **Millicent Martin, David Kernan, Gemma Craven**; 'Hello Dolly 1965 and 1979' with **Carol Channing and members of the company**
Noel Edmonds introduces 'The World of Disco and Rock & Roll': **Amii Stewart with Radford Quist, Charles Augins and The Norman Maen Dancers; Boney M – Marcia Barrett, Lis Mitchell, Maizie Williams, Bobbie Farrell; Bill Haley and the Comets**
Bernie Clifton
Vladimir Vasiliev, Ekaterina Maximova in a Pas de Deux from *Spartacus*
Les Dawson
Yul Brynner, Virginia McKenna and company in an excerpt from *The King and I*

1979

The 1979 Royal Variety Performance, presented for the first time by Louis Benjamin on his own, promised something different – and that was what the audience, including Her Majesty the Queen, got.

To begin with, after fifteen years at the Palladium, the 'royal show' switched to the Theatre Royal, Drury Lane.

The evening opened with actor Yul Brynner walking from the back of the stage in full evening dress to bow to the Queen and formally welcome Her Majesty to the theatre.

Much of the show was taken up with nostalgia: Ned Sherrin presenting 'Song by Song by Drury' - 'Showboat 1928' with Millicent Martin; 'Oklahoma 1947' with Julia McKenzie and the English National Opera Chorus; 'The World of Ivor Novello' with Hinge and Bracket. . . .

Solo music was provided by the imcomparable flautist James Galway, while Bernie Clifton, Les Dawson and Jim Davidson got many laughs.

The whole successful evening was rounded off in style with Yul Brynner and Virginia McKenna dancing a polka supported by other members of the cast of the successful musical *The King and I*.

Hinge and Bracket

1979

In his first 'Vice-President's Message' as presenter of the show, Louis Benjamin wrote in the programme:

> This, the 1979 Royal Variety Performance, is a rare occasion of 'firsts' – unique even for an event with such a long and distinguished history.
>
> It is – surprisingly – the very first time that the performance has been held at the Theatre Royal, Drury Lane, the oldest theatre in England and the very first 'Royal' Theatre.
>
> It is also the first Royal Variety Performance for most of the stars who will entertain you for two and a half hours or so tonight.
>
> Thirdly – and a 'first' of which I am particularly conscious and proud – it is the first time I have been honoured with the privilege of presenting and arranging the Royal Variety Performance.
>
> It is an exciting challenge. And the show devised sets out to embrace all aspects of entertainment – the past and the present, as well as looking to the future and the part to be played by entertainment in the ever-changing leisure habits ahead.
>
> We pay tribute to the magnificent contribution made to musicals over the years by the Theatre Royal, Drury Lane in a show format styled to fit the occasion, capture the mood and tempo of today and also acknowledge the changing facets of variety and musical theatre.

Bill Haley and the Comets achieved a 'first' of sorts in their rehearsal, which went down so well that they were asked to add an extra number to their performance on the night – usually artistes are asked if they can reduce the length of their material.

Virginia McKenna

Yul Brynner

Bill Haley

1979

The Queen for one was evidently delighted at the decision, and talking to Bill Haley afterwards she confided, 'You know, we grew up with you.'

The inclusion of the Bolshoi Ballet stars, Vladimir Vasiliev and Ekaterina Maximova, brought unexpected difficulties – not for the dancers who thrilled the audience with their performance, but for others concerned with their appearance in the show.

First was poor Louis Benjamin, who found himself the target of a group of highy militant Jewish ladies, vehemently opposed to the Soviet Union's policy on restricting Jewish emigration. From picketing the Coliseum when the Bolshoi were appearing there, they turned their fire on the Royal Variety Performance, calling on all Louis's years of tactful negotiation to mollify them.

On the other side of the coin came the near-farcical situation created on the night when James Mason came on stage to announce the two ballet stars and forgot their names! Recalling his acute embarrassment, he said, 'I was suffering from over-confidence because I thought I had those two difficult Russian names, so I didn't write them down on my fingernails. Then I got a block and there was no way out.'

Luckily, the leader of the orchestra was able to provide a timely prompt from the pit.

The million-selling pop group, Boney M, had to spend £2,000 on costumes as their stage clothes were reported missing *en route* from Rome. Their gear did eventually turn up, however, and they were left with two sets of clothes.

Red Buttons

Boney M

17 November
London Palladium
In the presence of Her Majesty Queen Elizabeth The Queen Mother
Presented by Louis Benjamin
Musical Director – Ronnie Hazelhurst
Producer – Norman Maen

THE PROGRAMME

THE LONDON PALLADIUM SALUTE
'In the Mood' – Joe Loss and his Orchestra
'Crazy Rhythm' with Una Stubbs, Lionel Blair and The Norman Maen Dancers
'Music Hall' with Roy Hudd, Arthur Askey, Chesney Allen and Billy Dainty, Charlie Chester, Charlie Drake, Arthur English, Cyril Fletcher, Richard Murdoch, Sandy Powell, Tommy Trinder, Ben Warriss
Paul Squires – Comedian (introduced by Stanley Holloway)
Bruce Forsyth
Grace Kennedy
Sheena Easton
Rowan Atkinson
The Wall Street Crash
Harry Worth Cleo Laine
THE HOLLYWOOD SALUTE
Henry Mancini
Peggy Lee
Victor Borge
Aretha Franklin
Sammy Davis Junior
Larry Hagman Danny Kaye

1980

This Royal Variety Performance had an added significance in that it was devised as a salute to the Queen Mother, who celebrated her eightieth birthday that year.

In planning it, Louis Benjamin and his colleagues planned a programme that spanned and reflected the very best in the field of light entertainment, from a nostalgic look back to the 1930s to the exciting tempo of the 1980s.

The evening got off to a perfect start with Joe Loss (himself seventy that year) and his orchestra.

After some 'Crazy Rhythm' with Una Stubbs and Lionel Blair, the theme switched to music hall. Those taking part in this wonderful extravaganza included the great student of the music hall and Chairman of the Entertainment Artistes' Benevolent Fund, Roy Hudd, and Arthur Askey, Chesney Allen (at eighty-six), Billy Dainty (who impersonated Allen's late partner Bud Flanagan), Charlie Drake, Tommy Trinder and so on – a marvellous tribute for the Queen Mother to savour.

There were also fine solo acts from Bruce Forsyth, newcomer Rowan Atkinson, Cleo Laine and Harry Worth.

The second half was devoted to 'The Hollywood Salute' with Sammy Davis Junior, by now a Royal Variety veteran, Peggy Lee, Larry Hagman and Aretha Franklin.

Larry Hagman

1980

Sammy Davis Junior

Lionel Blair was associate producer for the show and took the American side of the programme under his control. This included looking after Danny Kaye who announced that he wanted a microphone in the Royal Box, so that he could sing 'Happy Birthday' to the Queen Mother and she could sing back.

'To this day,' admits Louis Benjamin, 'I don't know if the man was serious. I never, ever found out.' Suffice it to say that Danny Kaye did not get his microphone, nor did he sing 'Happy Birthday' to the Queen Mother.

One of the high points of the evening was the sight of Larry Hagman dancing with his mother, Mary Martin. Thirty years earlier she had been the star of the legendary show *South Pacific*, in which, interestingly, Larry Hagman had appeared in the chorus.

One of the burning questions of the time was 'Who shot JR?' Not even the Queen Mother could prise the answer from Hagman, who maintained that his lips were sealed on the subject.

Mind you, his lips had been sealed on stage earlier in the evening when he dried during his sketch and completely lost his lines.

Roy Hudd was standing with Hagman's mother in the wings and heard her say, 'Jesus Christ, he's dried'; and then she went on to get him started again.

The audience loved this and to give him credit so did Larry Hagman. When it was suggested that the slight mishap could be cut from the television broadcast, he answered, 'No, you leave that in. The old girl got me out of trouble' – and in it stayed.

That year Roy Hudd regarded himself as 'the Shirley Temple of the outfit' judged against most of the other comics on the bill whose combined ages added up to a prodigious total (Stanley Holloway, making his last stage appear-

Rowan Atkinson

ance, alone was over ninety). They were all crammed into one dressing room which for the two days of rehearsal was almost constant bedlam with the likes of Arthur Askey, Cyril Fletcher, Sandy Powell, Tommy Trinder and Ben Warriss.

The noise in there had to be heard to be believed and even Billy Dainty who was the greatest talker of them all on his own couldn't get a word in. They talked solidly for four hours, then went down to the stage for a chorus of 'Strolling' and went home.

The next day it was the same story. Another four hours of non-stop joking and chatter, another chorus of 'Strolling' in the run-through and then back to the dressing room.

Half an hour before the start of the show silence fell and Billy Dainty, who had taken refuge in the shower to get changed, looked out and said, 'Thank goodness they've stopped, now perhaps they can think about what they're meant to be doing'.

At that moment the door opened and in came Charlie Chester who hadn't been to any rehearsals and they started again. Roy reckons they were still talking in the wings as the orchestra struck up the first note of 'Strolling'!

Left to right, from back: Roy Hudd, Richard Murdoch, Tommy Trinder, Chesney Allen, Arthur English, Sandy Powell, Ben Warriss, Billy Dainty, Cyril Fletcher, Charlie Drake and Arthur Askey.

23 November
Theatre Royal, Drury Lane
In the presence of Her Majesty Queen Elizabeth II
Presented by Louis Benjamin
Musical Director – Richard Holmes
Producer – Norman Maen

THE PROGRAMME

The Royal Welcome – **Robert Hardy**
'One Mo' Time!' – **Thais Clark, Vernel Bagneris, Sylvia 'Kuuma' Williams, Topsy Chapman, Patti Boulaye, Pearly Gates, Precious Wilson, The Clark Brothers, Kenny Lynch**
Dickie Henderson – The Host
Lenny Henry
Itzhak Perlman
John Inman and Guest
'25 Years of British Pop' introduced by **Tim Rice**, with **Lonnie Donegan, Marty Wilde, Acker Bilk, The Searchers, Donovan, Lulu, Alvin Stardust, Adam and The Ants, The Shadows, Cliff Richard**
'Covent Garden' with **The Norman Maen Dancers, Cambridge Buskers, Anita Harris**
Jimmy Tarbuck
'The Music of Andrew Lloyd Webber' with **Andrew Lloyd Webber, Stephanie Lawrence, Julian Lloyd Webber, Elaine Paige**
Mireille Mathieu and members of the *Bal Du Moulin Rouge* cast in 'The Can-Can'

1981

It was back to the Theatre Royal at Drury Lane for the 1981 Royal Variety Performance in front of the Queen. That fine actor Robert Hardy – possibly best known for his part in TV's *All Creatures Great and Small* – gave the formal welcoming speech.

This led on to the anything but formal celebration of black music with 'One Mo' Time!'

The evening was peppered with surprises, not least when *Are You Being Served?* TV star John Inman found his 'customer' was none other than the lovable former British boxing champ Henry Cooper. And astronomer Patrick Moore popped up to play, of all things, the xylophone.

The show was knitted together with his usual style by Dickie Henderson. A new star was born in comedian Lenny Henry, now a major TV performer in great demand. Pop music buff (and lyricist) Tim Rice introduced '25 Years of British Pop' with the likes of Marty Wilde, Acker Bilk, Lulu, Adam and the Ants and Donovan. And Tim Rice's partner on many hit musicals was featured in another slot – 'The Music of Andrew Lloyd Webber' - with the composer himself, his brother Julian on the cello and Elaine Paige.

A French finale came with the marvellous Mireille Mathieu and, of course, those gorgeous Can-Can girls.

Robert Hardy

Patrick Moore

1981

1981 saw another innovation, again stimulated by the need to counter the mounting costs of staging the Royal Variety Performance. For the first time sponsorship was introduced to pare down, in the words of EABF General Secretary, Reg Swinson, 'unavoidable ever-increasing production costs, as a prudent and acceptable alternative to increasing seat prices'.

The organizers also set out with the aim of raising the best part of £200,000 for the Fund from the night's show. In the end the figure was £209,000 – slightly more than double the return from the show of only two years earlier.

To quote Reg Swinson again, 'It was the hand of Louis Benjamin that wrought these fantastic results, he taking the initiative to increase the return on television fees, for the United Kingdom and overseas, the box office, brochure advertising and the introduction, in 1981, of sponsorship.'

There was almost what amounted to a royal exchange surrounding the appearance of the dancers from Paris. Earlier in the year Princess Anne had been invited as guest of honour at the opening of a new Moulin Rouge revue. When it came to planning the Royal Variety Performance, Louis Benjamin invited the Bluebell Girls to take part in the show and for the first time this century, the Moulin Rouge was closed, so that they could appear that night at Drury Lane. Although one of the most quintessentially French institutions, seven of the sixteen dancers in the Bal Du Moulin Rouge were English!

Donovan

Adam Ant

8 November
Theatre Royal, Drury Lane
In the presence of Her Majesty Queen Elizabeth The Queen Mother
Presented by Louis Benjamin
Musical Director – Ronnie Hazlehurst
Producer – Norman Maen
The Magical World of Musicals

THE PROGRAMME

The Royal Welcome – Richard Harris

Beginners Please . . .

Medley with Howard Keel, Helen Gelzer, Anna Dawson, Tony Adams, The Dancers

'Underneath the Arches' with Roy Hudd, Christopher Timothy, Joe Black, Peter Glaze, Tommy Godfrey, Billy Gray, Don Smoothey

Richard Stilgoe

'Bess You is My Woman Now' with Lesley Collier, Wayne Eagling

Great Musical Numbers

Introduced by David Jacobs, with Joyce Blair, Suzanne Danielle, Karen Kay, Aimi Macdonald, Ruth Madoc, Isla St Clair, Kenneth Connor, Leslie Crowther, Billy Dainty, John Inman, Pete Murray, Bernie Winters, John Hanson, Gloria Hunniford, Jan Leeming, Esther Rantzen, Vince Hill, Diane Langton, Lorna Dallas, Dennis Waterman, Anton Rodgers, Wall Street Crash, Topol, Liz Robertson, Tim Curry, Pamela Stephenson, George Cole, Bonnie Langford, Sylvester McCoy, Michael Praed, Chris Langham, *The Pirates of Penzance* company, Peter Skellern, Howard Keel, Jim Casey, Roy Castle, Eli Woods, Sheena Easton

Finale Please . . .

Moira Anderson, Buck's Fizz, Victor Spinetti, Amanda Redman, Robert Longden, The *Windy City* company, Jack Jones, The English National Opera Chorus, Angela Rippon and dancers from *Chorus Line*, Millicent Martin, Ethel Merman

1982

Musicals were the theme of the 1982 Royal Variety Performance, held for the third time in four years at the Theatre Royal, Drury Lane.

There were two reasons for this, explained Louis Benjamin. One was the Queen Mother's undoubted love for musicals and music hall, dating back many years. The other was that there had been two other very successful Royal shows in 1982 – one for children, the other for the Falklands Task Force's National Salute. Louis Benjamin said: 'Shows of this calibre, which reached such a wide television audience as well, used up a tremendous number of stars, thus making it increasingly difficult to find fresh RVP attractions and highlighting our constant awareness of the dangers of re-presenting the same formula over and over.'

This year, he said, 'we made the show the star'. After the Royal Welcome from actor Richard Harris there were performances from Howard Keel (on the very stage where he was virtually discovered), Anna Dawson and members of the *Pirates of Penzance* company; *Underneath the Arches* with Roy Hudd and others; 'Great Musical Numbers' with David Jacobs, Billy Dainty, Leslie Crowther and more; a 'music hall' memory with Jim Casey, Roy Castle and Eli Woods; *Windy City* with Dennis Waterman and Anton Rodgers, *Chorus Line* with Angela Rippon, and *42nd Street* with Millicent Martin.

Solo acts included the great Ethel Merman, Jack Jones and Sheena Easton.

Left to right, from back: Joe Black, Tommy Godfrey, Billy Gray, Don Smoothey, Peter Glaze, Christopher Timothy and Roy Hudd

1982

Esther Rantzen was one of an amazing trio of surprise singers. She was joined by Jan Leeming and Gloria Hunniford who astonished the audience when they burst into song. Perhaps it was not so much their harmonies that astounded but the outfits – they were all clad in cowgirl outfits. The song, by the way, was 'Anything You Can Do I Can Do Better' from *Annie Get Your Gun*. Esther was extremely modest about the group's contribution towards the music business, 'Our fingers are crossed, our legs are crossed and if we're still standing at the end it will be a miracle.'

Esther Rantzen

When Angela Rippon did her number she stopped the show. The following day a cartoon showing her doing her high kicks appeared in the *Evening Standard*. Louis Benjamin tried to buy this as soon as he saw it at eleven in the morning, but he was too late. The cartoon has already been sold – to none other than Angela Rippon herself.

Angela Rippon

One of the challenges in compiling a Royal Variety bill is to satisfy the constant demand for comedy. Louis Benjamin tried to make the point that you could have humour as well as comedy. There were very few pure stand-up comedians to be seen in the bill for the 1982 show, yet the show was a very big success both in the theatre and on television.

Jan Leeming

The high regard that is given the Royal Variety Show can be seen in the lengths that stars and impresarios go to in order to appear. David Merrick gave Millicent Martin the night off from performing in *42nd Street* on Broadway, especially to take part in the night's entertainment.

There could only be one fitting finale for this show and Ethel Merman provided it, flying in specially to storm on stage at the end to sing 'There's No Business Like Show Business'.

With one of the most celebrated stage entrances of all time, she was well able to

Millicent Martin

overcome a trifling physical detail that could well have thrown less accomplished artistes.

Sitting with the hairdresser before going on, she asked to have her hair all up at the front. But a quick look from the stylist showed that if Ms Merman's hair was all up at the front, there would be nothing to cover the back of her head – a point that she made as delicately as she felt she could.

'Honey, my name's Ethel Merman,' replied the great singer, 'and I've never turned my back on an audience in my life. So put it all up at the front and the hell with what anyone behind sees!'

Backstage, dressed in a terrible old dressing gown, she stumbled by mistake into the dressing room shared by a whole group of comics like Roy Hudd, Tommy Godfrey, Don Smoothey, Joe Black and Peter Glaze (of *Crackerjack* fame). She apologized, 'Oh, boys I'm sorry, I've got the wrong dressing room.'

'You'll be all right,' said Tommy Godfrey. 'You stay with us, darling,' and sat her on his knee.

'That's it, boys' she exclaimed. 'I'm dressing in here from now on!' – and she stayed there for ages talking about American vaudeville.

Ethel Merman

George Cole

Dennis Waterman

Sheena Easton

7 November
Theatre Royal, Drury Lane
In the presence of Her Majesty Queen Elizabeth II
Presented by Louis Benjamin
Musical Director – Alyn Ainsworth
Producer – Norman Maen
GOTTA DANCE!

THE PROGRAMME

Scott Sherrin
Gene Kelly – The Host
YESTERDAY'S TEMPO
Students of The Royal Ballet School, The Dancers, Bonnie Langford, The Frank and Kay Mercer Latin American Formation Team, The Jukebox Company Michael Barrymore
'Repercussions' with Wayne Sleep and The Dash Company
MUSIC HALL
The Dancers, Graham Fletcher, Sarah Kennedy, Fred Evans, Tony Kemp, Leslie Sarony, Billy Dainty, Merle Park, David Wall, Monica Mason and company in excerpts from *Elite Syncopations*
BROADWAY
The Dancers, Sheila White, Robert Wheeler, Gerry Zucarello, Grace Kennedy, Clarke Peters, Finola Hughes, Claud Paul Henry, The Roly Polys, Sheila O'Neill and members from the cast of *Kismet*, Gemma Craven, Jenny Turnock, Mary Corpe, Kay Townsend, Susan Hayes, Karen Berry, James Smillie, 'Miss World' Contestants, Julia McKenzie, Twiggy, Tommy Tune
TODAY'S TEMPO
Dee, Diana Moran, The British Amateur Gymnastics Team, The Dancers, The Rock Steady Crew George Carl
Bob Fosse's Dancin'
Pas de Deux from *Manon* with Natalia Makarova, Anthony Dowell
Les Dawson

1983

The 1983 Royal Variety Performance, like its predecessor, also had a theme – this year it was the world of dance.

From the moment when little Scott Sherrin self-assuredly opened the show, the evening set off at a fine tempo. The host was that master of dance Gene Kelly, in what was, astonishingly, his first Royal Variety Show. There was 'Yesterday's Tempo' with Bonnie Langford and others, and later 'Repercussions' starring ballet star Wayne Sleep and the well-named Dash Company. Dance on Broadway was also featured, and two star acts were Gemma Craven and Twiggy.

Adding humour to the frenetic pace were Michael Barrymore and the less-than-energetic Les Dawson.

The evening was a huge success – and it raised record amounts for the EABF.

Bonnie Langford and Gene Kelly

1983

Only eleven years old, Scott Sherrin had the honour of being the youngest person ever to have opened the 'royal show'. Although tender in years, Sherrin seemed impervious to the jitters which usually strike performers. 'I don't usually get very nervous but I expect there will be a few butterflies, just before I go on', he said.

Scott's act was a song and dance number from the film *Bugsy Malone*. His inspiration was a very famous Hollywood star: 'Gene Kelly is my idol', said Scott. 'I've seen every single film he's made.' And Gene Kelly was there to see Scott make his mark on one of the great institutions of show business.

Laurence Olivier was a surprise guest at this night's show. What may have seemed even more surprising was that the actor was asked to appear in a show which was honouring the world of dance. However, Sir Laurence showed his knowledge and appreciation of musicals and entertainers when he introduced Twiggy in a spot from her show *My One and Only*. 'It was a brilliant show, bristling with irresistible Gershwin melodies,' he told the audience, 'She [Twiggy] captured my heart entirely.'

He could have added that, for the first time in Broadway history performances were re-scheduled, so that Twiggy and Tommy Tune could fly to London to appear in the Royal Variety Performance. There was even one spectacular number that required a swimming pool, specially erected for the night!

During his act, Michael Barrymore snatched Mrs Beryl Low from the stalls to dance with him. Apparently, many people thought that she was a 'plant' in the audience, a misapprehension that was vehemently denied by Mrs Low, who stated, 'I am a fishmonger and I shall be back on my stall in Harlow tomorrow. I don't know what my customers would think if they knew. I just can't believe it.'

Twiggy and Tommy Tune

Michael Barrymore

19 November
Victoria Palace, London
In the presence of Her Majesty Queen Elizabeth The Queen Mother
Presented by Louis Benjamin
Musical Director – Ronnie Hazlehurst
Producer – Norman Maen
COMEDY TONIGHT!

THE PROGRAMME

'Comedy Tonight' with Leslie Crowther, Paul Nicholas, Bernie Winters, Billy Dainty, Jimmy Cricket, The Dancers, Mr Magoo, Brian Andro, Stuart Fell, The Acrobats
Master Anthony Gatto – Juggler Keith Harris
Denis Norden introduces 'The Bell Ringers' with Robert Dhery, Michael Bonnet, Gerard Coussine, Jean-Pierre Cassel, Jacques Gaffuri Les Dennis and Dustin Gee
'I Wanna Be Loved By You' with Angharad Rees, Matthew Kelly, Charlie Drake, Russell Grant
'Sonny Boy' with Frank Finlay, Simon Callow
'Sunny Side of the Street' with Eileen Atkins, Jean Marsh
Harvey and The Wallbangers Paul Eddington and members of the company of *40 Years On*
The Fabulous Tiller Girls
Ronnie Corbett
Galina Panova, Tim Flavin and members of the company of *On Your Toes*
Members of the cast from *West Side Story* in 'Gee, Officer Krupke'
Roy Hudd
Terry Wogan introduces James Galway, Henry Mancini
Last of the Summer Wine with Bill Owen, Peter Sallis, Brian Wilde
David Jacobs introduces Howard Keel
Paul Daniels
'Me and My Girl' – Robert Lindsay, Emma Thompson
'Flanagan and Allen' – Bernie Winters, Leslie Crowther
'Lambeth Walk' – Members of the *Me and My Girl* company

1984

After three years at Drury Lane, the Royal Variety Performance returned to the Victoria Palace for only the third time in its history.

The Queen Mother was treated to the theme of 'Comedy Tonight' – an appropriate theme in a theatre where the Crazy Gang had starred for many years. And the warm-up, from Barry Humphries, Eric Sykes and Spike Milligan, was in Crazy Gang style. And later, Bernie Winters and Leslie Crowther starred as Flanagan and Allen.

Roy Hudd, Paul Daniels and Ronnie Corbett, all well-used to Royal Variety Shows, showed their mastery of comedy on the stage, while two young comedy stars Robert Lindsay and Emma Thompson performed with members of the *Me and My Girl* cast.

The evening had the best possible end when Max Bygraves serenaded the Queen Mother.

1984

It probably came as a consolation to young performers to find that even a comic as seasoned as Roy Hudd can get just a tiny bit jittery about appearing in a Royal Variety Performance. In 1984 he went on to deliver a marvellous monologue by Keith Waterhouse and Willis Hall about a policeman walking home off-duty when he passes Buckingham Palace and sees a girl running across the courtyard minus one item of footwear 'to wit – a glass slipper'. It was a wonderful piece and went down extremely well, particularly with the Prince of Wales who said to Roy Hudd after the show, 'Don't laugh, I know policemen like that.' All of which made the twenty circuits Roy made of the Victoria Palace as he went through his lines more than worth the anxiety.

Backstage, Spike Milligan was in great form in his dressing room, telling stories and joking with friends. The only distraction to the constant flow of Milliganisms was the tannoy carrying the show up from the stage, but Spike soon dealt with that, ripping it from the wall and then saying, 'Right – maybe I can get to the tag of this one now.'

At the presentation after the show, he asked the Prince of Wales whether he had enjoyed the show, adding, 'I've had a word with the missus. She said she enjoyed it.'

The heir to the throne said that he had enjoyed the show very much as well.

When the time came for the Royal party to leave, Prince Charles said to Spike, 'Goodbye Milligoon.'

'Goodbye, trainee King', called Spike as the prince walked away.

'You're for the tower, Milligan,' he said, turning with a huge grin, before leaving to join the princess.

Jimmy Cricket

Eric Sykes, Matthew Kelly, Charlie Drake and Spike Milligan

1984

Constructing an all-comedy show is not as easy as it may seem, or as the ratings suggest (this one went straight to number one). There's no telling how things will go, and for the presenter and director the worst aspect is running time, which can go seriously awry without a firm hand – even if it feels like a wing and a prayer at times.

As with all Royal Variety Performances there was great good will and support in this one. Writing in the programme, Louis Benjamin remarked, 'For instance, in what business, other than show business, would you phone all the way to Australia to ask such a celebrated personage as Dame Edna Everage to do a mere ninety-second spot and get an instant "Delighted, Possum" from Barry Humphries? Or get so many big names who usually take the stage for fifty minutes or more, settle for just one minute or two and in the case of one particular star – who will be witnessed if you watch the Royal arrival closely – agree to appear without actually doing anything or saying anything!'

Robert Lindsay and Emma Thompson

The wonder of technology made it possible to view Torville and Dean's latest dance routine. The ice dance number was recorded in Australia and transmitted to the show via satellite. The skaters flew over especially (although not by satellite) to be introduced to the Royal Party.

Anthony Gatto was one of the youngest artistes to be asked to appear at the Royal Variety Performance. A precocious juggler, Anthony twirled hoops and batons almost as big as himself.

The audience must have wondered if they were seeing things as they scanned the Royal Box. Dame Edna Everage, housewife superstar, was holding court there and had to be persuaded to vacate the premises.

Eric Sykes with Dame Edna Everage

Theatre Royal, Drury Lane
In the presence of Her Majesty Queen Elizabeth II and The Duke of Edinburgh
Presented by Louis Benjamin
Musical Director – Alyn Ainsworth
Producer – Norman Maen
THE WORLD OF FILM MUSICALS

THE PROGRAMME

THE EARLY YEARS

42nd Street – 'Audition', **Karin Baker, Randy Skinner**

Babes on Broadway with **Danielle Carson and Michael Howe** portraying Judy Garland and Mickey Rooney

Showboat with **Iris Williams**

****

Gary Wilmot

****

THE SCREEN GODDESSES

Sarah Payne portrays Betty Grable

Rula Lenska portrays Rita Hayworth

Gloria Hunniford portrays Doris Day

Stephanie Lawrence portrays Marilyn Monroe

****

Rolf Harris

****

1985

THE GOLDEN YEARS
The Show Dancers
Jean Simmons
'Sit Down, You're Rockin' the Boat' from *Guys and Dolls* with **David Healey, Betsy Brantley, Norman Rossington**
On the Town with **Tim Flavin, Graham Fletcher, Peter Alex-Newton**
Elisabeth Welch
'Triplets' portrayed by **Michael Aspel, Jan Leeming, Russell Harty**
'We're in the Money' from *42nd Street* with **Philip Gould**
Alice Faye
Roy Castle portrays James Cagney
Fred Evans
****
Anna Neagle
****
THE BRITISH YEARS
Doreen Wells and Tudor Davies portray Anna Neagle and Michael Wilding – 'Spring in Park Lane'
Ron Moody – *Oliver*
Sarah Brightman portrays Jessie Matthews – 'Evergreen'
Norman Wisdom – 'Trouble in Store'
Su Pollard portrays Gracie Fields – 'Sally'
THE POST-WAR YEARS
Joan Collins
'The Social Dance' from *Seven Brides for Seven Brothers* with **Roni Page, Steve Devereaux**
High Society with **Celeste Holm, Paul Nicholas**
'Lullaby of Broadway' from *42nd Street* with **Frankie Vaughan, Barbara King**
'Are You Lonesome Tonight?' – **Martin Shaw, Simon Bowman**
Liz Robertson – 'On a Clear Day'
'The Night They Invented Champagne', from *Gigi* with **Beryl Reid, Amanda Waring, Geoffrey Burridge**
'A Couple of Swells' – **Dennis Waterman, Maureen Lipman**
West Side Story – **José Carreras**
THE FRED ASTAIRE YEARS
The Show Dancers in 'Let Yourself Go', 'The Bandwagon' and 'Let's Face the Music and Dance'

1985

Once more the Theatre Royal, Drury Lane played host to the Royal Variety Performance.

The Queen and Prince Philip watched as the theme of 'Film Musicals' unfurled before them. In fact, so complete was the theme that no less than five top West End musicals – *Guys and Dolls, Gigi, Seven Brides for Seven Brothers, 42nd Street* and *Are You Lonesome Tonight?* all closed for the evening so performers could take part in the 'royal show'. There were some great performances – Su Pollard of *Hi-de-Hi!* fame as Gracie Fields; Gloria Hunniford as Doris Day and Stephanie Lawrence as Marilyn Monroe, while a star of musicals today, Sarah Brightman, was outstanding as Jessie Matthews. An undoubted favourite of the night was the wonderful Ron Moody as Fagin in *Oliver*.

The list of stars was virtually endless: Joan Collins, Beryl Reid, Jean Simmons and a number of surprise appearances, including Patrick Duffy (Bobby Ewing in TV's *Dallas*) and Lauren Bacall.

One of the highlights of the night was Dennis Waterman and Maureen Lipman as 'A Couple of Swells', which brought some of the biggest applause of a very successful night.

An exciting moment for Su Pollard

1985

There was an intriguing cameo role for actress Rula Lenska at this performance. She portrayed Hollywood star Rita Hayworth, singing 'Put the Blame on Mame' from the film *Gilda*, which she prepared for by watching clips from the film a good many times.

The big headache for the presenter was finding a theatre large enough for 1985's Royal Variety Performance. The Victoria Palace – at which the show had been held the previous year – had 800 fewer seats than the Palladium or Drury Lane and Louis was desperate to find a larger theatre. Having dinner at the Savoy one evening with David Merrick, he took the bull by the horns and asked him, 'How about shutting the theatre [Drury Lane] for a week to let us do the Royal Variety Show?'

To his amazement David Merrick looked him straight in the eye and said, 'Yes.'

Bearing in mind that *42nd Street* was an early musical film, this set the ball rolling for the idea of this year's theme. Since it was so easy to use the resident show, two pieces were taken from *42nd Street*. And on to these, and other numbers from large musicals, were grafted the impressions of famous movie stars moving almost through a chronology of the film musical.

One of the most hilarious moments of the evening came from Wayne Sleep and his dancing partner doing a wonderful send-up of Torville and Dean as they pretended to skate on the stage. Once again Louis Benjamin had had to struggle to include this against the demands for more orthodox comedy. His judgement was sound once again, and the two dancers got more laughs than many stand-up comedians. There were people in the audience in tears with laughter.

Rula Lenska

Gary Wilmot

1985

For Louis Benjamin this was his last year as presenter. In six years he had transformed the financial position of the Royal Variety Performance, and by extension that of the Fund, but the cost of staging something as spectacular and intricate was rising each year and the time looked ripe to pass the torch to the television companies who now played a crucial role in the success of each year's show.

'It was doubly fulfilling for me,' he readily acknowledges. 'To have the privilege of doing them and to have helped the Fund out of difficulties.'

It may not be known by many people outside the profession that Joan Collins's father was the well-known agent, Joe Collins. One member of the cast who certainly did know it was Peter Elliott, one of the EABF committee, who was in the line-up at the rehearsal for the finale and called over to the star of *Dynasty*, 'Eh, Joan, your father owes me £200 commission.'

'Well, you won't get it from me,' answered the lady.

Joan Collins

1985

Stephanie Lawrence

24 November
Theatre Royal, Drury Lane
In the presence of Her Majesty Queen Elizabeth The Queen Mother
Presented by BBC Television
Musical Director – Ronnie Hazlehurst
Director – Norman Maen
Producer – Yvonne Littlewood

THE PROGRAMME

The Royal Welcome – **Peter Ustinov**
WHEN IT ALL BEGAN – 1936
The Royal Variety Dancers
Alan Randall portrays George Formby
Su Pollard and Ruth Madoc portray Gert and Daisy
Kit and The Widow portray The Western Brothers
Marti Webb portrays Gracie Fields
Bob Monkhouse
Marti Caine
Angela Rippon
Petula Clark
Rory Bremner
Peking Opera
Victoria Wood
The Bluebells
Carolyn Pickles
Stephane Grappelli
Nana Mouskouri

1986

Victor Borge
THE GOOD OLD DAYS
Frank Carson, Valerie Masterson, Max Bygraves
ENTR'ACTE
'Top of the Pops' – Lulu with The Royal Variety Dancers
Michael Davis
Ronnie Corbett
Paul Nicholas, Nicholas Parsons and members of the company of *Charlie Girl*
Paul Daniels
FIFTY YEARS OF DANCE
Lesley Collier and Stephen Jefferies
Peggy Spencer and the Latin American Formation Team
Cyd Charisse and members of the company of *Charlie Girl*
Simon Howe and members of the company of *42nd Street*
'Cagney and Lacey' – Tyne Daly, Sharon Gless
****
Ken Dodd
****
THE MUSIC OF OUR LAND
Huddersfield Choral Society
The Pipes and Drums of the 1st Battalion The King's Own Scottish Borderers
Val Doonican
Gloria Hunniford
Aled Jones

1986

As the year which marked the fiftieth anniversary of television broadcasting by the BBC, it was highly appropriate that 1986 should mark the first year in which BBC Television presented and arranged the whole of the Royal Variety Performance for the Entertainment Artistes' Benevolent Fund.

In celebrating half a century of television broadcasting there was a strong combination of stars of television and of more traditional stage acts.

The Queen Mother, warmly received after her recent illness, was treated to a surprise TV 'transplant' with the cast of the BBC's *Only Fools and Horses* starring David Jason.

Humour was in plentiful supply with Ken Dodd, Bob Monkhouse, impressionist Rory Bremner, Victoria Wood, Frank Carson and Max Bygraves.

Song came from Petula Clark, the youthful Aled Jones, Val Doonican and Nana Mouskouri.

And television was an important part of the show with the stars of the American cop-girl series *Cagney and Lacey* – Tyne Daly and Sharon Gless – going through their paces on stage.

But there was nostalgia too, with Alan Randall in his brilliant impression of George Formby, Kit and the Widow as the Western Brothers and Marti Webb as Gracie Fields.

Peter Ustinov, that most relaxed of performers, gave the Royal Welcome, while the finale with pipes, drums, bands and Val Doonican, Gloria Hunniford, Aled Jones and a surprise appearance by Dame Vera Lynn was a suitably rousing end.

Left to right: Paul Daniels, Sharon Gless, Tyne Daly, Ronnie Corbett, Max Bygraves and Bob Monkhouse

1986

Angela Rippon's was the act that everyone wanted to see but it only happened once in a decade! She at last repeated her famous high-kicking dance routine, ten years after she startled the world by appearing in the Morecambe and Wise show and disproved the myth that newscasters exist only from the waist up.

The controversy surrounding jokes about the Royal Family raged on in 1986. Singalonga-Max Bygraves was determined to keep in his joke about Princess Michael of Kent. 'I'll do it, I'll do it,' he vowed. Michael Grade, Controller of the BBC had other ideas. 'It won't get through. You just don't make jokes about the Royal Family.' Max was keen to have the last word, 'People forget that the Royal Family have a sense of humour. I might even think of a better joke overnight.' Whether he did or not was academic. Strict protocol still prevailed.

Victoria Wood

Rory Bremner

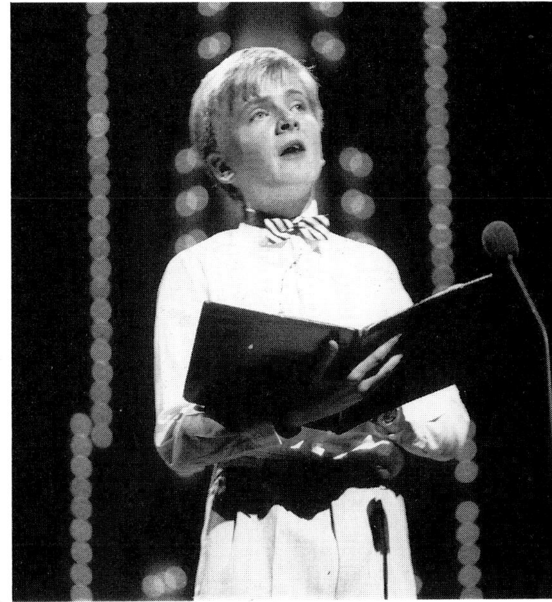

Aled Jones

23 November
London Palladium
In the presence of Her Majesty Queen Elizabeth II and The Duke of Edinburgh
Presented by London Weekend Television
Musical Director – Alyn Ainsworth
Producer – David Bell

THE PROGRAMME

Anthony Newley and The Alan Harding Dancers
'Ghosts of the Theatre' with Jessica Martin, Gary Wilmot, Peter Goodwright, Hilary O'Neil, Allan Stewart, Bernie Winters, Leslie Crowther
George Carl – International Speciality Bobby Davro Dolores Gray from *Follies*
Les Dawson and The Roly Polys
Johnny Logan Cannon and Ball
Shirley Bassey
Five Star Ronn Lucas
Dudu Fisher, Kaho Shimada, Michael Maguire and members of the cast from *Les Misérables*
Stephen Fry and Hugh Laurie – Comedy Masterclass
Eartha Kitt
Hale and Pace
James Galway introduces Alan Brind, Evelyn Glennie, Vladimir Ovchinikov
Mel Torme and George Shearing
Michael Barrymore
The Phantom of the Opera excerpt with Sarah Brightman
Mike Yarwood Johnnie Ray Rosemary Clooney
Harry Secombe Jimmy Tarbuck
Tom Jones

1987

The Queen and Prince Philip enjoyed a mixture of nostalgia and modern show business at the 1987 Royal Variety Performance at the Palladium, presented this year by London Weekend Television.

Nostalgia came early, in the 'Ghosts of the Theatre' spot. Bernie Winters and Leslie Crowther played Flanagan and Allen, Allan Stewart was the incomparable Sir Harry Lauder, while Jessica Martin was Judy Garland. Contemporary humour came from two of the brightest comedy stars of the moment, Stephen Fry and Hugh Laurie. Other comedy came from Michael Barrymore, Jimmy Tarbuck, Cannon and Ball and the newer act of Hale and Pace as dinner-jacketed 'hard men'.

There was much music to delight the audience, provided by artistes like James Galway, Shirley Bassey, the sensual Eartha Kitt, and an extract from the *Phantom of the Opera* with Sarah Brightman.

Hale and Pace

1987

'Tonight's show,' wrote Brian Tesler, the Chairman and Managing Director of London Weekend Television, in the Foreword to the Performance, 'takes the Palladium itself as its theme and will contain some nostalgic reminders of the great stars and shows that have graced this magical stage over the years. The nostalgia will be particularly heady for those of us who worked here in the earliest years of Independent Television on the celebrated *Sunday Night at the London Palladium*, which appeared in ITV's very first weekend on the air back in 1955. I was fortunate enough myself to be the show's producer for some of those exhilarating early seasons, and I am personally delighted that the close links between ITV and the theatre continue to be maintained – again on Sunday nights – with LWT's weekly series *Live From the Palladium*.'

Firm believers in self-censorship, Stephen Fry and Hugh Laurie cleaned up their act to save the Queen from any embarrassment. Out went a four-letter word and a joke about sex. 'We don't necessarily believe Her Majesty would take offence but we would hate to cause her any embarrassment,' said Stephen Fry.

Understudy of the evening award went to Richard Branson, Virgin tycoon. He stood in for Jeffrey Archer as Eartha Kitt's companion as she sang her distinctive song 'Old-Fashioned Girl'.

Shirley Bassey won universal admiration when she appeared at this year's show, her first major engagement since the death of her daughter two years earlier. Her return to the stage was deemed to be a hit of the show.

Stephen Fry

Hugh Laurie

Five Star

The Roly Polys

21 November
London Palladium
In the presence of Her Majesty Queen Elizabeth The Queen Mother
Presented by BBC Television
Musical Director – Ronnie Hazlehurst
Producer – Michael Hurll

THE PROGRAMME

The Band of the Scots Guards, The Royal Variety Dancers, The Hornchurch, Rainham and South Hornchurch Majorettes
Ronnie Corbett, Bruce Forsyth – The Hosts
Mickey Rooney, Ann Miller from *Sugar Babies*
The Chong Qing Troupe
Brian Conley Kylie Minogue
The cast from *Neighbours*
Mel Smith and Griff Rhys Jones
Cliff Richard
The cast of *Bread*
The world according to . . .**Jackie Mason**
Julio Iglesias
'Pop '88' with **Bananarama, Rick Astley, A-Ha**
From Hollywood, *The Golden Girls* with **Bea Arthur, Betty White, Rue McClanahan, Estelle Getty**
Bob Monkhouse
From Broadway, **Michael Feinstein**
Bruce Forsyth and Ronnie Corbett
Russ Abbot with Bella Emberg
Paul Daniels presents 'The Greatest Show on Earth' with **Debbie McGee and Stars of British Circus**

1988

Perhaps as never before television had a massive impact on the content of the 1988 show at the Palladium held before the Queen Mother.

The cast of the Australian soap *Neighbours* appeared, as did the cast of BBC's *Bread* and the stars from the American show *The Golden Girls*.

But, for many, the big hits of the evening were the more traditional acts such as stand-up comic Jackie Mason, singer pianist Michael Feinstein and the comedy duo of Mel Smith and Griff Rhys Jones as scenery movers. Not only was the show counted a success it also, unlike some previous performances, ran to time.

Mel Smith and Griff Rhys Jones

1988

As Chairman of the EABF, Roy Hudd was invited this year to open the show for the television audience, setting the scene in the foyer of the Palladium as the audience were arriving. This captured the excitement and anticipation of the occasion perfectly and offered Roy an ideal opportunity to explain the work of the Fund and its long association with the Royal Variety Performance. The only difficulty was finding a suitably quiet corner to record this and Roy eventually ended up positioned outside a door marked 'Gentlemen'. It required five takes before they managed to shoot him without the unscripted appearance of one of several men innocently coming out while he modestly 'adjusted his dress'!

The Chong Qing acrobatic troupe from China were one of the distinctive features on the bill. They performed quite impossible feats flying through hoops and climbing poles with singular aplomb and dexterity. 'Unbelievable, but wonderful,' commented *The Stage*.

The tradition and longevity of the 'royal show' were joked about by Mel Smith and Griff Rhys Jones. The Queen Mother and Princess Margaret were especially amused when they were obliquely referred to, 'The Royal Variety has been going since 34 BC . . . it was first put on for Queen Boadicea. But she couldn't get there, so her mother and sister went instead.'

Rumours that Kylie Minogue did not get on with her former colleagues were dispelled by her warm introduction to them, 'Now I would like to introduce you to some very good friends of mine, the cast of *Neighbours*.'

Mickey Rooney and Ann Miller appeared in a song and dance routine from their show *Sugar Babies*. They belied their total age of over 120 years to give a marvellous performance.

Kylie Minogue

Paul Daniels

1988

As one reviewer commented, 'Together with the luscious long-legged Ann Miller – her too 'Darned Hot Spot' in *Kiss Me Kate* will never be forgotten – Mickey resuscitates the spirit of American vaudeville. Superb! The pair of them.'

The close of the performance was certainly unusual, ending as it did with a spectacular circus finale hosted by Paul Daniels, with confetti and sparkling gold dust raining down on the stalls and balloons cascading from the roof. As one commentator remarked, scenes like this are commonplace at political rallies in the USA, but it was the first time that the audience at a Royal Variety Performance had seen anything quite like it.

Ann Miller and Mickey Rooney

1988

Rick Astley

A-Ha

Bananarama